Many books of diverse kinds hav
but I cannot think of one which explores with such insight the
importance, the gentle beauty, the challenges and the demanding
realities of loving others, loving self and being loved. Love, in all
its manifestations in our lives, can enrich and enable each of us.
Fr O'Donnell sets out myriad ways in which we may live in love
and with love, knowing that we, too, are loved. It seems to me to
be the product of decades of work and observation, of scholarship
and of an ability to analyse some of the most difficult, wonderful
and complex circumstances of life, taking the reader into the many
facets of love, the consequences for those who live without love,
and the healing and joy-giving experience of receiving love, and
of giving love. In this book, which is easy to read, Fr Desmond
O'Donnell has given us an opportunity to know a little more the
meaning and the mystery of love. It is well worth reading.

Baroness O'Loan

*To Love and to Be Loved* provides a rewarding exploration. Full of
insight and experience, of what it is to love in a rapidly changing
world. Desmond O'Donnell brings together an army of writers
who have thought deeply about the subject and melds them
into an exposition that is personal, profound, and abounding in
practical suggestions. It is a book that cannot fail to deepen our
understanding of a concept that is as mysterious as it is familiar.

David Crystal, Editor of *The Cambridge Encyclopaedia*
*of the English Language*

This book is a delightful accessible read, introducing people to the important topic of love and friendship. At the centre is an explanation of the language of love, in the Bible, both in the Old and New Testaments. A particular strength is the variety of insights drawn from poets, scientists and philosophers, to name but a few.

Fáinche Ryan, Professor of Theology at Trinity College

Again Fr Des O'Donnell has provided us with a work of rare brilliance. Those of us who know Des well will discern in *To Love and to be Loved* the fruits of a lifetime of wise reflection, wide reading, deep prayer, and an energetic love for others and for God. But those of you who know Fr O'Donnell only as an author will also find yourselves truly enriched and greatly blessed.

✠ Richard Clarke. Church of Ireland Archbishop of Armagh

This is a wonderful, encouraging and wise book which rests on a very wide scope of understanding – and scholarship – and I felt I gained so much insight into my own life in reading it. There is so much that I like about it but I found especially rewarding Fr O'Donnell's emphasis on the role of encouragement in both giving and receiving love, and how even a small measure of encouragement can mean so much in a person's life. The author's compassionate understanding of those he has counselled is matched by his knowledgeable reading of spiritual texts – and also drawing on sources from Viktor Frankl to the iconic words of Humphrey Bogart in *Casablanca*. Every page is filled with something golden and inspiring.

Mary Kenny, playwright, author and journalist

Yes, as the title suggests, love is the great driving force in all of our lives. It is at once uplifting and joyful, baffling and mysterious. We rarely find words that adequately do justice to this most profound of human experiences – love. Des O'Donnell has written a book that probes the mystery of love by building on his wide experience of its expression in so many human situations. Equally, he backs up his experience with a wide scholarship on the subject. He writes wisely and with great empathy for all our limitations when it comes to understanding this vast subject. I recommend this book to anyone looking for new insights or who simply needs confirmation of their personal experience of love

✠ Willie Walsh, Bishop Emeritus of Killaloe


At a time when hate speech, xenophobia and fake news are coarsening political discourse and widening divides, it is a pleasure to read the wise words of Fr Des O'Donnell, showing us the power of love. He reminds us that love is the most profound of human experiences, and his scholarship draws on writings over the centuries to prove it.

Mary Robinson, former President of Ireland

In his book *Bowling Alone*, published in 2000, Robert Putman called attention to the problem of increased solitary living and loneliness in the developed world.

Eight years later, Bill Bishop published *The Big Sort: Why the Clustering of Like-Minded America Is Tearing Us Apart*. In it, he describes the increase of groups which share narrow religious or cultural views and which thrive on anxiety-laden assemblies of fearful people.

This year, John Kasich published *Two Paths: America Divided or United*. In it, he encouraged the love-your-neighbour theme, without any religious underpinning. He describes the problems of loneliness and selfish grouping as cultural ones, without saying how they can be solved.

The aim of this book is to show that the solution to both of these problems is within us.

To Love and
to be Loved

*'Take away love, and the earth
becomes a tomb.'*

Robert Browning (1812-1889)

*Desmond O'Donnell* OMI

# To Love and to be Loved

DOMINICAN PUBLICATIONS

First published (2017) by
Dominican Publications
42 Parnell Square
Dublin 1

ISBN 978-1-905604-35-7

British Library Cataloguing in Publications Data.
A catalogue record for this book is available
from the British Library.

Cover design by David Cooke

Printed in Ireland by
SPRINT-print, Rathcoole, Co. Dublin

Re-printed February 2018

# Contents

# Dedication

*I dedicate* To Love and to be Loved
*to my beautiful parents, Susan and Seamus,*
*to my worldwide Oblate family*
*and to all my friends,*
*who by their loving presence in my life*
*have made me who I am.*

# Foreword

'What is this thing called love?'
'What! Is this thing called love?'
'What is this thing called? Love?'
Whatever way these six words are arranged or punctuated, they all pose a basic question about the meaning of authentic love. The theme of love is of universal interest and has always been so. Some 52 million people use dating apps such as Tinder each day seeking someone to love them, according to *The Economist* (13 February 2016). Before speaking of parental love, of friendship-love, of partnership-love or of love in marriage, it would seem essential to think about the deeper meaning of all love. This book is about that deeper meaning.

The life of every person on our planet has been influenced by the presence or absence of love, whether they are aware of it or not. Older people know that the experience of being loved is as life-giving as the air we breathe, even though we are generally not consciously aware of either. Psychologists affirm that the presence – conscious or unconscious – of love in our lives is vital for full human living.

From the first moment of conception, a baby is so enveloped in the life-giving love of the mother's womb that it does not even have to make an effort to breathe. Later, the shock of leaving the security and warmth of the womb, of having to breathe unaided and of having to confront changes of temperature and levels of noise is lessened and made endurable for the baby by the loving touch and warmth of the parents' bodies. Ideally, this loving continues until parents die, having enabled their children as they developed to love and care for others.

The theme of love has inspired much of the beautiful literature, art and music in human history. Over the ages, many of the most noble acts of which people are capable have been inspired by love. We think of people who risked and sometimes gave their lives out of love for others, in families or in simple friendship. We think of the Polish priest, Maximilian Kolbe, who stepped forward at Auschwitz and gave his life in the place of another prisoner who had a wife and children. In modern times, the generous service of Médecins sans Frontières and the violent deaths that some of them have suffered, remind us that selfless loving is not a thing of the past.

Past generations did not need to reflect on love in their personal lives. They enjoyed it without analysing it. At the same time, some people endured close living which lacked love and they stayed together because of public expectations or church rules. Things have changed. In a short time, the developed world has moved from a culture of authority to a culture of choice. For good or for evil, a tradition-based culture has become a present-directed one. Much social scaffolding has disappeared, and many once socially-supported relationships which might have been called love, have become brittle. With the new stress on personal freedom, and less on endurance, what was taken for granted about relationships cannot be presumed anymore. People have gradually adopted a malleability in the way they live and relate to others.

Modern life in the Western world makes the question about love, and about all relationships, more urgent. As personal mobility increases, as connections between people become more fragile, and as the question of personal identity is now a really challenging one, the meaning of love has become a central issue for reflective individuals and groups.

External norms have been replaced by inner gyroscopes in guiding most peoples' lives. As a result of this, friendships seem to fracture more easily. Loneliness increases. In 1950, sociologists Riesman, Glazer and Denny wrote a book called *The Lonely Crowd*. It is considered to be one of the most influential books of the twentieth century and now psychologists speak about loneliness or alienation as the pathology of our age.

Sadly, the word 'love' has been used as a label to describe despicable acts of inhuman behaviour, such as rape and child abuse. Since the 1960s, the word 'love' has sometimes been misused in otherwise inspiring films or interesting TV programmes to describe infidelity or maltreatment of people. Maybe this is why enjoyable and inspiring love stories are becoming less frequent. In many situations, love has sometimes become disconnected from words like 'respect', 'fidelity', and from any enduring human relationship. Family therapist and film reviewer Frank Pittman wrote in the *Networker*: 'The word love can be used to defend spouse shedding, romantic adventurism or orgasmic smorgasbords. So many people do not understand that these activities can never become stabilizing reality exercises. They seem destined to hover around the fringes of real love for ever'. At the same time, real love is still copiously visible in the world today. Most of us have received it from our parents and friends. We receive it and we pass it on in our families and in other relationships.

The beautiful aspect and expression of love in sexual intercourse has often been identified with the totality of love; but now, even its connection with love is losing ground. For some people, sexual intercourse seems to have taken on a life of its own: it has become a pleasurable pastime, disconnected from any commitment to a permanent relationship.

Technology has facilitated progress immensely in so many ways; yet we must note its inability to deal with the most central aspects of human life, such as hope, anxiety, joy, peace, goodness, beauty, honour, striving, suffering, weakness, gentleness, trustfulness and self-control. Nevertheless, any treatment of love must consider the influence of the Internet on the quality of human communication.

The practice of loving does not depend on religious faith but real faith adds a unique dimension to love. This dimension is dealt with directly in five chapters at the end of the book. Scripture quotations are taken from the New Revised Standard Version.

The big question remains; how do we recognise authentic love? This book tries to answer that question. It is also an effort to describe the rewards that love brings, and the non-negotiable demands it makes. Hopefully it will encourage many people to keep on loving, some to love even more deeply, and others to begin loving despite some hesitancy after past hurt.

CHAPTER ONE

# *The Wisdom of Loving*

WE CAN inherit wealth but not wisdom. Wisdom is developed over many years, through personal experiences and through contact with wise people. Hopefully, parents are the first wise people from whom we learn. As we grow, wisdom has to be won through listening to many other wise people, through hearing about their experiences and through reflecting on them. Over the centuries, wise people have had much to say about love.

In the tenth century BC, Solomon, the famous king of Israel, wrote: 'Many waters cannot quench love. Neither can the floods drown it' (*Song of Songs* 8:7). It would appear that he describes love as a dynamic movement which, if authentic, has the power to conquer all that opposes it.

In the eighth century BC, the prophet Micah offered this formula for happiness: 'This is all that God asks of you, only this, that you act justly, love tenderly and that you walk humbly with your God' (*Micah* 6:8)

In 60 BC the Latin poet Virgil wrote: 'Love conquers all things. Let us too, give in to love'.

While talking with a Buddhist monk in Sri Lanka Buddhism, I pointed to a few ants climbing on his saffron gown, expecting that he would brush them off. He noticed my concern and said, 'They are beautiful, aren't they? About 2,500 years ago, the Buddha called his followers to love every living thing. He had this to say about love: "Uncovered, the eye will see, unblocked the ear will hear, and unencumbered the heart will love".'

The long tradition of Buddhist thought and practice is encouragingly telling us that love is not a command that we must obey. It is, rather, a privileged source, a wellspring within us, calling us to use it. Our hearts are made to love, as our eyes are made to see and our ears to hear. It is only when our eyes and ears are blocked, covered or damaged that they are unable to exercise their normal function of seeing and hearing. The human heart wants to love, and it will automatically love unless it has been damaged or prevented from doing so in some way.

Born about 6 AD, Jesus said that love is the life-link between God, himself and his followers: 'I have loved you as the Father has loved me' (*John* 15:9). And 'Love one another as I have loved you.' (*John* 13:34).

Here he is reminding us that the experience of being loved by God is a dynamic source of energy enabling us to love others. Whether we experience that love of God directly or through those who love us, receiving enables us to pass it on to others.

Writing to believers in Corinth in the first century, Paul of Tarsus summarized his teaching in these words: 'Now faith, hope and love remain, these three, but the greatest of these is love.' (*1 Corinthians* 13:13) He also assures the Colossian Christians that 'Love binds everything together in harmony.' (3:14)

Philosopher and theologian Augustine of Hippo (354-430), having lived a reckless life and fathered a child outside of marriage when he was just 18, eventually wrote his famous Confessions in which we find him stressing the aesthetic aspect of love: 'In as much as love grows within your soul, does beauty, because love is the beauty of the soul.'

English mystic, Julian of Norwich (1342-1416), in *Revelations of Divine Love*, wrote: 'It is love alone which gives meaning to all things.'

In *The Anatomy of Melancholy*, the English author, Robert

Burton (1577-1640), who taught at Oxford, also wrote about the power of authentic love: 'No cord nor cable can so forcibly draw, nor hold so fast as love can do with a twined thread.'

John Stuart Mill (1806-1903), English philosopher and social reformer, wrote in his autobiography: 'Those only are happy who have their mind fixed on some other object than their own happiness; on the happiness of others, on the improvement of others. Aiming thus, they find happiness by the way.'

Congregationalist minister and antislavery activist Henry Ward Beecher (1813-87) wrote in his autobiography: 'I never knew how to worship until I knew how to love.'

Without using the word 'love' in his book, *A Splendid Torch – Elise*, George Bernard Shaw (1856-1950) speaks about it:

> This is the true joy of life, to be used for a purpose recognized by yourself as a mighty one; being a force of nature instead of a feverish, selfish little clod of ailments and grievances, complaining that the world will not devote itself to making you happy. I am of the opinion that my life belongs to the whole community; as long as I live, it is my privilege to do for it whatever I can. I want to be thoroughly used up when I die, for the harder I work, the more I live. I rejoice in life for its own sake. Life is no brief candle for me; it is a sort of splendid torch which I have got hold of for a moment, and I want to make it burn as brightly as possible before handing it on to future generations.

In his *History of Western Philosophy*, philosopher and mathematician Bertrand Russell (1872-1970) stressed the same point when he wrote: 'Man is a social animal. As long as social life survives, self-realization cannot be the supreme principle of ethics.'

Jewish philosopher, sociologist and theologian, Martin Buber

(1878-1965), in his famous book *I and Thou*, wrote: 'Existence will remain meaningless for you if you do not penetrate it with active love, and if you do not in this way discover its meaning for yourself'.

Geologist and palaeontologist Teilhard de Chardin (1881-1955) spent his life on the study of human prehistory and humanity's relationship with the universe. His research convinced him that, despite our occasional inability to love beyond a select few, there is such a thing as universal love that is still evolving. Because of this growing focus on universal love he said that every human cell in the world is striving towards unity with all the others. He forecasts, in *The Divine Milieu*: 'The day will come when, after harnessing the ether, the winds, the tides and gravitation, we shall harness for God the energies of love; on that day, for the second time in the history of the world, we will have discovered fire.'

After years in clinical practice, social psychologist and psychoanalyst Erich Fromm (1900-80), famous for his work on motivation, said that his experience of human growth had taught him this: 'It is not he who has much that is rich, but he who gives much.' He also wrote: 'Giving is the highest expression of power. In the very act of giving, I experience my strength, my wealth, my power. This experience of heightened vitality and potency fills me with joy. I experience myself as overflowing, spending, alive, hence very joyous. Giving is more joyous than receiving, not because it is a deprivation, but because in the very act of giving lies the expression of my aliveness'

A theologian who based his theology on anthropology, Karl Rahner (1904-80), wrote (text in *A Rahner Reader*): 'Saying no to loving imprisons the whole person within the deadly lonely damnation of self-created absurdity. Loving the other is not just something which also exists in us – one talent among many others, but it is the fullness of each of us in his or her total achievement.'

The Jewish psychiatrist Viktor Frankl (1905-73) was professor of psychiatry and neurology in the University of Vienna. In *Man's Search for Meaning* he wrote: 'The meaning of life is having someone to love, something to achieve and a sense of the good, the true and the beautiful. Love is the ultimate and highest goal to which a person can aspire. The salvation of man is through love and in love.' Because he lived by this belief, Victor Frankl survived the Auschwitz concentration camp while his wife and his brothers were being wiped out by the Nazis.

Dag Hammarskjöld (1905-61), winner of the Nobel Peace Prize, who generously lived out the primacy of love as Secretary General of the United Nations, and who died on one of his missions, described his own life in the following words (*Markings*): 'It is so simple; always live for others. Never seek selfish interests.'

In her book, *A Simple Life*, Mother Teresa (1910-97), champion of the poor, wrote: 'The greatest disease in the West today is being unwanted, unloved, uncared for. We can cure physical diseases with medicine but the only cure for loneliness, despair and hopelessness is love.' She also wrote: 'Success is in the loving; it is not in the result of loving'. She is telling us that love is effective whether it has obvious results or not.'

Speaking about everyone's need for freedom, Pope John Paul II (1920-2005) wrote, shortly before his death: 'The worst prison would be a closed heart.'

Black minister and civil rights leader Martin Luther King (1929-68) lived a life of love for his marginalized people, and was killed as he struggled for justice. He said this in *Strength to Love*: 'Love is the most powerful force in the whole universe, and it is also the most available because everyone can tap into it anytime'. He also left us with this radical thought: 'Life's most important question: what are you doing for others?' and this radical challenge: 'Every man must decide whether he will walk in the light of creative altruism or in the darkness of destructive selfishness'.

In 1983, in his well-known book *The Road Less Travelled*, popular writer and psychiatrist Scott Peck summarized his clinical experiences and his personal wisdom in this way, when he wrote:

> The experiencing of real love also has to do with ego (i.e. self-boundaries, since it involves an extension of one's limits. One's limits are one's ego boundaries. When we extend our limits through love, we do so by reaching out, so to speak, towards the one loved, whose growth we wish to nurture. What transpires then in the course of many years of loving, of extending our limits of our cathexis (i.e. attraction, investment, commitment) is a progressive enlargement of the self, an incorporation within of the world without, and a growth, a stretching and a thinning of our ego boundaries. In this way, the more and the longer we extend ourselves, the more we love, the more blurred becomes the distinction between the self and the world. Real love is a permanently self-enlarging experience and it is in giving up of self that human beings can find the most ecstatic and lasting, solid and durable joy of life.

In 1999, American moral theologian, Charles Curran, who edited *The Development of Moral Theology*, had this to say about loving others: 'Morality is the mystery of the claim of the other'.

In 2014, for the World Apostolic Congress on Mercy, German theologian Walter Kasper wrote: 'Personal existence is constituted by relationships with other persons.' Here he is stressing what modern humanistic psychologists are saying, that a person is fully a person only in relation to others, that the fullness of personhood exists only in interpersonal loving. He is also saying that freedom to love others overrides the person's need for exclusive self-interest. There is always a tension between self-protection and self-gift, which tests our ability and our freedom to love.

In 1947, to a farmer who asked him for wisdom to pass on to his son, Einstein replied: 'Nothing truly valuable arises from ambition or from a mere sense of duty; it stems from love and devotion towards others'. He also wrote: 'Only a life lived for others is a life worthwhile.'

# CHAPTER TWO

# *Parental Love*

MANY years ago, when families were larger, I saw a lady hustling seven or eight children into a tram in Melbourne. Thinking of the reduced rate for groups, the conductor asked her, 'Are they your own or is it a picnic?' She smiled graciously and replied, 'They are all my own and I love every one of them, but, brother, it's no picnic'.

Among the most significant developments in psychology and psychiatry has been the steady growth of evidence that the quality of caring love which a child receives from its parents, or from its mother- or father-figures, will be of vital importance for the remainder of its life. In the first years, the baby is defenceless, almost totally dependent on parents. This fact has been enhanced by a still deeper discovery, namely that the security a baby feels in the womb has an enduring effect on its entire life. As children grow, their defences become stronger. However, the need for nurturing and protection lasts well into adolescence.

If satisfaction of these early needs has been lacking, the result will be deprivation. Depending on how severe the deprivation has been, the child will have less physical, mental, emotional and social resilience. Increased vulnerability and some unhealthy anxiety can then become part of the person's life. Hereditary factors can influence the degree to which some children can survive or overcome this. We do not yet understand the exact effect of our genetic history; the relative importance of nature and nurture still remains to be determined. While counselling and some form of psychotherapy can help, the result of deprivation rarely fades fully. We are sure, however, that love given in the womb and in early life is the best start that a child can have for a healthy later life.

These facts make parenthood a demanding way of life. However, when there is deep caring coming from authentic love, parenthood becomes one of the most rewarding and enjoyable experiences known.

A baby's experience of closeness to its mother is crucial for development. If a mother is at peace with herself, happy to carry her baby and free of excessive stress, the womb is the perfect place to supply the baby's needs for nourishment, comfort and security. The birth experience is a moment of great deprivation for a baby until its need for the warmth of human contact is felt again by the tender welcome of its mother's embrace. Minutes after birth, the baby recognizes its mother's voice because it has become accustomed to hearing it in the womb. Very soon some babies search for a human face, and can respond with a smile especially at the mother's breast, even in the first few weeks after birth.

This smile says, 'I feel loved'. When this moment has not taken place, difficulties can arise in the child's development. Babies receive love through warm touch, cuddling, being kissed, being smiled at and being fed. Babies are not consciously aware of love, but they thrive as they receive it, and they decline when it is absent. In technical language, we are 'hominized' in the womb, but we are 'humanized' by love. Being loved makes us whole.

The baby's growing feeling of self-worth gradually enables it to understand the world around it, to make judgements about it, to resist impulses, and to acquire self-confidence by exploring, by taking initiatives, and by achieving little tasks. This development of internal security is most important in order to develop the ability to relate well to other people. This sense of confidence in oneself is imperative. As Henry Ford, in his book *My Life and Work*, wrote: 'Whether you think you can or whether you think you can't, you are right.' This love prepares the child for the dramatic changes of puberty and the challenges of adolescence, when even parents' love can be severely tested at times. Loving parents provide the child with a refuge from too much stress that might inhibit this growth. Together with teachers, parents also become a source of wisdom during this time when children are subconsciously interiorizing the values that will guide them throughout their adult lives.

In his book *The Art of Loving*, the renowned psychoanalyst Erich Fromm says: 'All these experiences of being cared for become crystallised and integrated in one experience – I am loved for who I am or I am loved because I am'. This is a passive, subconscious experience, but it responds to the almost pressing need of most children up to the age of about eight to ten: of being loved for what one is. Strangers can teach a child what *things* are, but parents teach who *they* are. A loved child will learn and never unlearn that to have a place in a parent's heart is never to be alone, especially when life roughs them up at school or elsewhere.

In the early years, a child does not love; it responds with happiness to the enjoyment of being loved. Later the child thinks of giving love to the parent, of producing love by its own activity, by giving small gifts or doing something that pleases its parents. Children do this from mixed or maybe selfish motives, but gradually their relationship with their parents is being transformed from merely being loved to giving love. People gradually cease to be primarily a means of satisfying the child's own needs. Without this transition, the young adolescent will become a selfish, demanding person, unless counselling or therapy can change attitudes later. Without the transition from the enjoyment of being loved to that of giving love, young people remain in danger of never becoming a loving spouse or a successful parent

Encouragement is the most powerful motivation in helping a child to grow; sarcasm is the most harmful. To grow, children must learn to investigate and to be adventurous. Unless there is danger in their reaching out, the loving, growth-enhancing thing to do is to help and reassure them as they continue to venture into the changing world. It is best to allow children to make mistakes rather than to do everything for them. One seldom finds that people attain anything unless they have first gone astray. In short: never limit your children to your own learning; they have been born for today, and must learn to live in a tomorrow when you are gone. Do not call them to where you are, as beautiful as that place may seem to you. You must have the courage to let them go to a place where neither you nor they have been before.

Use of the word 'we' is always fruitful, because it communicates love and the indispensable feeling of togetherness and belonging. Likewise, using the words 'no' or 'later', when necessary, gives children borders and helps them to develop the impulse control that will be an essential part of their lives if they are to live harmoniously with others and form relationships A river without banks becomes a swamp. All children need boundaries even though they sometimes resist them vigorously.

The words 'keep trying' are helpful if a child tends to give up on a useful task. Because real-life situations do not respond to the touch of a smartphone, some enduring effort in the face of adversity is always part of successful living. If parents always surrender to a child's 'I want it, I want it all, I want it here and I want it now', or to 'I cry and I get', they are preparing their child for a very frustrating future. Adults know that much of life involves effort and struggle, and even if they are on the right track they will be run over unless they move forward. As Alexis Carrel has written in his book, *Man the Unknown*: 'Degeneration of body and soul is the price paid by individuals and races who have forgotten the law of struggle, albeit mental, moral or physical'. Success is a ladder, not an elevator, and a diamond is a chunk of coal that made good under pressure. Loving parents help their children to learn this. Otherwise, their children are being hardwired for an unhappiness that thinks life is effortless. They don't always give their children cut flowers; they teach them to grow their own, and to wait while they grow.

Catching up was easier in the past, but much that is good in modern life demands the effort to keep up. A child's desire to investigate, to create, to keep up and to learn, is strong, and gentle help enables the learning process. Parents, however, must wait while their children learn rather than do things for them. To love is to understand, and to understand is to wait. Parents should answer their children's questions with as much information as they need at the time, and recognize that most children are full of 'whytality', without really needing perfect or detailed answers.

It is important that children's manual dexterity and intelligence grow, but it is just as important that they develop their sense of the aesthetic, their appreciation of music, art, literature and all things beautiful. On the journey of life, parents need to teach their children to stop off at islands of beauty - to enjoy scenery, visit an art gallery, or help arrange a vase of flowers.

When most of us think of love in the form of fairness, caring and patience, we think of our parents. We think too of the pain we caused them. Perhaps we also recall ways in which our parents failed through impatience or by angry words when they were tired. Parents may have failed us by disagreeing between themselves in our presence. However, we know that their goodness lives on in every good act we do, and we are grateful. In a deep sense, our parents taught us not just to be good children but to become good parents ourselves for the next generation. Grandparents enjoy observing this growth in action.

We all have to learn that fragility, futility and falling are part of life. Every child must be taught that if something is worth doing the only response to failure is to get up once more often than one falls. And loving parents need to remind themselves that occasional failure on their part will not be permanently harmful. Loved children are very resilient. It is not so much a parental programme that determines a child's future; it is the unique world in which they are surrounded by their parents' love. Children grow mostly by what they observe, absorb and feel, more than they do by what they hear or by what they are commanded to do.

Single parents, parents with a special-needs child, or a parent whose partner takes little interest in helping their children all inspire us, as their love is tested in a special way.

We have seen that every child needs a home, but they also need a horizon: they need faith or a gradual introduction to God who, like a good parent, encourages, forgives and inspires them. Faith itself cannot be passed on from parents to children, but the disposition or openness to receiving faith can be fostered in them. By being warmly loved, by learning that he or she can trust, by growing in the ability to share and to be grateful, the readiness for faith is gradually created in the child's feelings.

When children feel warmth, security and gratitude in the words 'Mammy' and 'Daddy', they are gradually becoming ready to receive faith. Thoughts and explanations come later. Jesus taught adults, but he hugged children.

When God chose words to describe divine love, he chose 'Father' and 'Mother'. Jesus said: 'How often I have desired to gather your children together as a mother hen gathers her brood under her wings' (*Luke* 13:34). God is our loving, caring, supporting father and mother.

CHAPTER THREE

# *Loving in Modern Life*

PEOPLE are always influenced by the culture in which they live, and they change as it changes, for good or for ill. Rapid cultural change is bringing a new situation in which we need to look again at the experience of loving and of being loved. The past 60 years have probably seen the greatest social and cultural change in human history. Those events certainly touched those of us who grew up in and lived through the changes, but they also affect those born into them.

As far back as 1958, in his book *The Sane Society*, the well-known social psychologist Erich Fromm wrote this:

> Modern man has transformed himself into a commodity; he experiences his life-energy as an investment with which he should make the highest profit, considering his position and the situation on the personality market. He is alienated from himself, from his fellow men and from nature. His main aim is profitable exchange of his skills, of his knowledge and of himself, his personality package with others who are equally intent on a fair and profitable exchange. Life has no goal except the one to move, no principle except the one of fair exchange, no satisfaction except the one to consume.

In a changed culture, people will love and must be loved differently. Modern life puts new pressures on loving because life today has become participation in a fast-changing process. This process of constant change and the emergence of a 'me' generation calls for more demanding ways of loving for which many people seem unprepared.

'If we speak about love in contemporary Western civilization we must ask whether its social structure and its dynamics make it conducive to the development of love or tends to oppose it'. This was also addressed by Fromm in his much published work *The Art of Loving*. He also wrote that, in the place of real love, 'many forms of pseudo-love' have begun to exist. He explains this by saying that a capitalist society which forces people to be 'on the move, to function and to get ahead', has reduced love or caring to a market commodity in many places and in many lives. We can see this when marriage looks like becoming a bargaining experience, where one partner sells and the other buys to the satisfaction of both. This market approach seems to work until one partner becomes dissatisfied with his or her side of the bargain.

In today's massive cultural flux, modern individuals may or may not be wiser than their parents, but they certainly have more information, more questions, more choices, and the need to make more instant decisions. People today are more mobile geographically as they travel more. They are also more mobile mentally as they grow increasingly diverse in their opinion of what is important. Even traditional sources of identity-strength are drying up. The question, 'Who am I?', has become more urgent than in the past when people led less hurried and more predictable and stable lives. Levels of self-harm through anxiety and over-work, or through over-indulgence in food and alcohol, or through drug-taking and suicide, were much lower. Anxiety levels have increased in every developed country.

Most modern people have high demands on personal well-being and so they are pulled towards guarding their free time carefully. If two people agree on how to spend their free time or when one of them is prepared to have less freedom for the sake of the other, then love can flow smoothly. But when the demand for freedom becomes too highly personalized, love is on trial. A husband whom I was counselling said that his wife was 'high maintenance', meaning that he considered that her needs were becoming excessive. Because they generally have to work hard, modern persons treasure their free time and increase their demands. There is a stronger demand for 'having fun' and people have no hesitation in demanding their sometimes very different descriptions of fun. When two experiences of fun are identical, loving can be easier; but when they differ, love will be tested.

Most counsellors agree that loneliness is growing. Many psychologists have gone so far as to say that alienation is the illness of our time. Some serious illnesses can have their origin in this lack of connectedness, in the absence of feeling cared for, in this scarcity of love. In the past, people did not move house as often as they do nowadays. People knew their neighbours by name, and they met one another more frequently. This closeness made stable love easier. But now, frequent house-moving, demanding jobs and busy lives lead to anonymity and to aloneness. Friendship and love are nurtured by closeness. Distance often makes them more demanding.

Individuals' self-awareness and consciousness of their distinct selfhood have grown in recent years, and this is surely a good thing. At the same time this knowledge increases consciousness of their rights. Consequently, people are not as ready to let go of their rights as they were in the past. This attitude is a good thing, but again it puts new demands on the selflessness called for in loving. Emphasis on an individual's rights puts more and more demands on self-giving and the patient loving of the other. The person who continually stresses his or her rights needs to realize that less emphasis on rights gives space for more loving, while stressing them could indicate a growing selfishness.

In the past, people were given overall meaning for their lives by parents and by society. Meaning was more easily transmitted to children in an authoritarian way, often with emphasis on religious motives. Values and vision were often mildly forced upon us. There was little room for questioning, little room for expressing doubt or disagreement. Commands were accepted passively even if they were not obeyed in practice. This gave boundaries and meaning to life, and it held families, social groups, neighbourhoods and even cultures together, in spite of great odds and even with manifest injustice. Today, authority and directives are much less effective as social glue. Consequently, loving and mutual caring have now become more a choice and less a command. This makes them both more authentic and perhaps more difficult.

There is another need for emphasis on love today: when they are free, people now tend to put greater emphasis on personal choice than on commands or on guidance from outside. Laws come from outside of us and are more effective when they are accompanied by rewards or with a threat of punishment. Society needs these. But when laws fail to motivate or to control selfish behaviour, people need something else to keep social life pleasant. We might call this a sense of responsibility. When rules and sanctions become less effective in making life together successful, only real caring or love will make it so.

People are beginning to feel powerless before economic and political forces. Election promises are often not kept. Salaries sometimes do not meet basic needs. Inefficient and sometimes dishonest banking causes people's hard-earned money to disappear. Even homes are often lost. Trust has lessened in bankers, politicians, big companies and church leaders. This loss of trust increases a feeling of disconnectedness in most people today. At the same time, it is bringing people together even in simple gestures such as job-sharing or car-sharing and in major events like responding to flooding or family bereavement. Many are gradually beginning to feel that the effort to live and to do things together is more enriching than to struggle alone. The importance of love – perhaps inspired by what is mutually beneficial – is now beginning to emerge more strongly in many places.

Being loved helps to protect us against many social pressures such as the force of advertising. While the advertising world helps us to know what is available, many of its activities are aimed at parting us from our money. Spoken and written messages are directed at increasing our desire to control and to consume. Many people tend to spend more than they can afford, and their families have suffered because they could not resist the latest commercial must-have item. People now need to build up their resistance to commercials. A good feeling of self-worth enables us to say 'What I have is enough', and to distinguish between our needs and our desires. When people have the support of mutual love they can discuss their everyday pressures, and build up the strength to resist the subtlety of advertisements and the demands of the acquisitive instinct.

Because individuality is increasingly stressed today, life together with a common purpose to achieve worthwhile goals is difficult. Yet, lessening individual needs and goals is becoming more necessary if individuals or groups are going to survive. Every time we purchase what we do not need, we increase its market value and its cost for very poor people. Our willingness to be aware of the needs of others and to love people whom we will never see is becoming an urgent necessity. The same is true if our own groups are to maintain social cohesion, and continue lessening the gap between the rich and the poor. The decision to be lovingly concerned about the other's welfare sometimes leads to at least a moment of personal inconvenience, and for this reason only love, even for people whom we will never meet, can motivate it.

To say 'forever' to another person, or to a way of life, as in marriage or in religious ministry, is very difficult today. We often hear statements like 'I'm keeping my options open.' Decisions become 'for the time being', and life promises are sometimes made carelessly. In the presence of these mindsets, no laws, no rewards or sanctions can ensure fidelity to promises. In modern culture this is understandable, even if it is not ideal. Situations are changing rapidly today; and because of the ever-present avalanche of information, individuals too are changing their values, goals and hopes more easily and more often than before. Only commitments based on real and radical love can ensure fidelity. Love is now becoming an island in a whirlpool of throw-away relationships.

Modern life tends to encourage a false autonomy that stresses 'me' and my needs, and emphasizes immediate satisfaction. People who succumb to this trend cannot love perseveringly. They can only market and exchange their personality packages for the short term, and live desperate, lonely, loveless lives. The press of a few keys on Facebook enables a person to type in the words 'I love you', and to send this message dishonestly or mean-inglessly to any number of people with whom they will never exchange a gift, may care about, and will probably never meet.

The increasing stress of work, resulting in partners returning home over-tired each evening, is testing the quality of their love and is leading to more broken relationships. Increased mobility is also putting demands on close relationships. It will continue to do so until people gradually recognize the need for some regular quiet time together, no matter how difficult it is to arrange this.

In his letter, *Laudato Si'*, Pope Francis describes the stress which the media can put on friendships today:

> When the media and the digital world become omnipresent, their influence can stop people from learning how to live wisely, to think deeply and to love generously. Real relationships with others, with all the challenges they entail, now tend to be replaced by a type of internet communication which enables us to choose and eliminate relationships at whim, thus giving rise to a new type of contrived emotion, which has more to do with devices and displays than with other people and with nature. Today's media enable us to communicate and to share our knowledge and affections. Yet, at times, the media also shield us from direct contact with the pain, the fears, and the joys of others and from the complexity of their personal experiences. For this reason, we should be concerned that, alongside the exciting possibilities offered by these media, a deep and melancholic dissatisfaction with interpersonal relations or, a sense of isolation, can also arise.

# CHAPTER FOUR

# *To Be Loved*

ALMOST everyone has had some experience of having been loved, perhaps in childhood, and, hopefully, through later life into adulthood. If you have true friends, you are loved. And each time you meet a friend, you are both changed. It is like mixing two chemical substances: they blend and they both are changed.

To be fully human, we need to have loving relationships in our lives. We are not self-made; we are made by being loved. We receive that love first in a womb, then in our family, from our relations and later from friends. In his book *Rickshaw Boy*, Chinese novelist Lao Tzu wrote, 'Being loved by someone gives strength, while loving someone deeply gives you courage'. Loving and being loved are always an enrichment. Deep in all of us, there is the question, 'Will someone cry when I die?'

People who have lived together in physical closeness grow in sensitivity about the presence or absence of love in their lives. Living in a family or in a partnership can gradually increase the experience of love received. On the other hand, a stressful situation arises if, while living near others, a person feels that he or she is not loved. Just observing older married couples can tell us much about love. In Sonnet 104, Shakespeare wrote: 'To me, fair friend, you can never be old, / For as you were when first your eye I eyed, / Even such seems your beauty still.' There is no antique like an old friend.

In preparation for writing this chapter, I found it useful to listen to the experience of a number of people, male and female.

Part of my interviews included asking each person to complete either or both of these unfinished sentences:

When I am sure that I am loved, I know that …

When I know that I am loved, I feel …

Most responses used the words 'happy' and 'great' until I pressed the interviewees to be more descriptive by using a few sentences. Seven of them wrote a paragraph describing a way or a time in which they were aware of being loved. I think that these paragraphs describe the experience well.

A woman who struggled with a low image of herself, put it like this:

> When I am sure that I am loved, I grow in my feeling of self-worth. Because I am gay, my young years were lonely. My relationship with another woman who is also gay increases my respect for myself because another person has thought me worth loving to the degree of living with me. My friend has decided to gift me with her love by living with me, by doing many things for me and sharing her life freely. This enables me to feel and to grow in self-worth. I feel sure that I am growing more beautiful.

Genuine love received is always a gift, a growth-giving experience. This free gift of love can be anything from a friendly smile, a well-chosen present, an invitation to a shared meal, time given listening to another, or lives totally shared. In each of these we experience being cared about to some degree, and we receive a message telling us that we are of value. This silently increases our feeling of self-worth and self-respect. It also increases our capacity to love others.

A reflective older Canadian man wrote of being loved as a privilege received:

I know that when I am given love, the loving action is given to me uniquely. It is not for anyone else. Such is my wife's and my family's love for me first of all, and then that of many others. The love I receive is always a privilege given to me. Of course I am not always consciously aware of this.

One cannot think like this every time love is received, but – subconsciously and sometimes consciously – every time one is shown love there is some feeling of being special, of being permanently privileged, even if it is only for a passing moment.

Receiving love almost always gives joy to the person receiving it, but knowing that the giver enjoys giving it adds still more joy to the person who receives it. Thomas Merton stressed that love is its own reward. This experience is like having the sun shine on one from both sides. It seems to describe the experience of this young Australian woman who, like so many others, relished her parents' love:

> When I think of the love my parents and my siblings have for me, the only word I can use to describe the feeling is 'treasured'. This feeling increases when I am aware of how much joy my love gives to my father and mother each time I Skype them, but especially when I return home. Some-times it makes me feel bad about all the times I made life difficult for them during my adolescence.

Giving love is always a pleasant experience, but sometimes it can demand sacrifice. Receiving love, which clearly demands inconvenience or sacrifice from the one who gives it, enriches the experience of being loved. An older lady whose cancer had become serious, wrote:

> My discomfort and anxiety are growing and I think I could

bear it only with the support of my wonderful husband. I look back over the last three years during which he has cared for me when I was not in hospital. The love I received, and am still receiving, comes through great sacrifices and from the pain and anxiety he shares with me at this time. His daily sacrificial love increases my love for him, and I reflect on it every night as I fall asleep.

One simple and unmistakable sign by which we know that we are receiving love is when we are supported. We all need support most of the time and some of us need it all the time. A young man during his final year in secondary or high school said this:

> Teachers are busy, hardworking and usually kind people. I have about average intelligence, and, like a few of my friends, I struggle academically. One teacher gave us special attention and even extra time after school. She supported our sometimes faltering efforts. Our adolescent emotions at the time were leading to some confusion about love, but now, on reflection, I am sure that Aoibhin's time-consuming love not only helped us academically, but it gave us the experience of being loved beyond the confusing emotional, sexual feelings we were going through – even those we were feeling towards our attractive teacher.

Love received gives energy and clarity that otherwise we might not have.

Speaking up for someone against a mistaken perception or during a false accusation – especially in a group – is love given, and surely the experience of love received by the person being defended. A wife and mother told me that on one occasion, when her husband accused her wrongly, her six-year old son spoke out, saying: 'Daddy, you are wrong'. She told me how happy she was, not because she was declared innocent or because the child had the courage to speak, but that she experienced the love her little boy had for her.

Encouragement is the strongest motivation in helping anyone. An older man wrote this:

> During the early days of my marriage, partially through my own fault I ran into serious financial difficulties. Having to sell our home seemed the only option. Our very dear friends next door shared our anxiety and stress but they could not help us financially. Day after day they told us how they would miss us if we had to go. They encouraged us and found some extra work for my wife and me. They kept telling us how they were praying for us and had others doing the same. We often sipped out the problem over a pint with them until my wife and I began to feel that we were indispensable to our neighbours. In the end we succeeded in staying in our home. We still live with and reflect on the intense feeling of being loved by being encouraged throughout our crisis.

Psychologists recognize that to belong to a caring group is a vital experience for human growth, and even for survival. This is generally true also in most of the animal world. The lone elephant is dangerous in his loneliness. In Jaffna, in northern Sri Lanka, I saw a small refugee village partially trampled into the ground by such an elephant.

A young Chinese man who had an early experience of drug-taking and drug-trading, wrote about how the experience of belonging had saved him:

> After mixing with some druggies I began to take some lighter drugs and then to peddle them. I was arrested, and

charged in a minor court. My fellow druggies assured me that I would not be punished for a first offence – which was true. Presuming this, I had little intention of giving up my wayward behaviour as I entered that courtroom, but the sight of my father and mother there too changed me. Their presence and look of love on their faces assured me that I belonged. Today I am a successful small businessman.

I also see in the experience he describes a prime example of the saying that 'only those who love us can change us'.

Love is not blind. In fact, because it is willing to see more it is willing to see less. Real forgiveness is so much easier when we know the whole story of the offenders, when we see more. Their offence against us may be obvious and may seem unforgivable. It is only when we love that we can look more deeply at the offenders, at their insecurity, their fears, their anxieties and above all their lack of human development due to their defective upbringing, and see the whole picture. Love alone can look deeply. Love looks and listens with the heart. Only with this quality and depth of love can we turn condemnation and the desire for revenge into forgiveness. Bad manners, unkind deeds and hurtful remarks can often be a lonely cry for notice or for help; only love can discover when this is true. Almost all of the people I interviewed said that, when they were deeply loved, they were sure of frequent forgiveness, and that each time they were forgiven, they grew in appreciation of the other's love for them.

Love constantly received can sometimes be taken for granted. To avoid this occurring here is a very humanizing and growthful practice that takes about one minute before one falls asleep. Try to reflect back on the times people showed us kindness during the day. Perhaps it was in a smile, a gift given, help offered, an act of patience or forgiveness, an encouraging word or a listening heart or perhaps just having been wished well, or a promise to pray for you during the day. This is an enriching experience especially if you can re-live how you felt after each of these loving moments. Then, it is equally enhancing to name the moments when we ourselves freely showed love to others. Every day which we end by reflecting on a few of these love-received and love-given moments is a good day, and any day lacking all of them is a sad day indeed, because love received is always also life received. And, of course we love best when we know ourselves loved.

American novelist Raymond Carver has two of his characters say:

And did you get what you wanted from this life even so?
I did.
And what did you want?
To call myself beloved, to feel myself beloved on the earth.
('Late Fragment', from *A New Path to the Waterfall*)

And in a discussion on poverty, the poet and playwright William Butler Yeats asked: 'Who being loved is poor?'

How do you personally accept love? Your answer to this question will help you discover in what way you do.

If someone you know well, said to you 'I love you' what would you spontaneously reply? Write your response here or elsewhere.

.......................................................................................................................

.......................................................................................................................

.......................................................................................................................

You will be able to evaluate your response later in this book (see Appendix, pp. 165-166).

—

# CHAPTER FIVE

# To Love Is to Feel with

FEELINGS and emotions[1] are deep and difficult to describe. Our actions are what we do; our thoughts are what we think; our values are what we believe in; but in some way our feelings are what we *are* experiencing at any time. In *Faith and Feelings edited by Lonergan*, Christopher Friel describes feelings as 'the mass and momentum, power and drive of human existence'. For our purpose here they can best be described as pleasant or unpleasant sensations which influence our experience of life much of the time. They can bias our thinking towards truth or untruth.

Some examples are feelings of joy, sadness, shame, elation, guilt, embarrassment, depression, happiness, loneliness, strength, vulnerability, and of being loved, lonely, hesitant, confident, afraid, anxious, peaceful, depressed, weak, strong, angry, friendly, tired, energetic or helpless. These feelings can have different depths and different durations and can be present singly or in very complex groups. Generally, they are also fairly unpredictable. They always arrive without invitation and are not under our direct control in the sense that they cannot be commanded to come or to go. They have a life of their own influenced by bodily chemistry and external influences.

Feelings are essential to healthy living, and so they are useful.

---

1. Feelings and emotions are not the same. Feelings are more basic. Emotions are more complex. Loosely, feelings give rise to emotions, e.g. the feeling of very hot water gives rise to the emotion of anxiety. The feeling of loneliness can cause the emotion of fear. Yet the words are often loosely equated, as they are in this chapter.

Without them life would be barren and unmanageable. Pleasant emotions, like peace and joy, encourage us to enjoy life, and to be more productive. Negative ones like anxiety or fear warn us of danger. There is an emotional illness identified by almost total lack of feeling. It is called sociopathy, and afflicted people are called psychopaths. These are people who lack feeling to a significant degree. They may know when they are acting wisely, fairly, unwisely or unjustly, but their choices of how they behave are not being reinforced by feelings. This emotionless experience can lead to actions that are dangerous to those afflicted and to others. When external stress like a job loss enters a marriage, mutually warm feelings can hold that marriage together. On the other hand, a low calibre emotional life, that is, an inability to feel deeply, can lead to irresponsible behaviour by neglect of duty or by harmful activity like marital infidelity.

Often enough we hear another say to us, 'I know how you feel'. Sometimes it means that he or she thinks that this is true. It may indicate that our friend would like to share our feelings of sadness or of joy but we cannot always be sure how far the speaker actually senses our feelings. In fact, it is psychologically impossible to feel the identical feelings of another with exactly the same degree of intensity. Our individual uniqueness does not allow this to happen, despite the presence of deep concern for the other. When we know that our friends actually do share our feelings, even in part, it is a consoling experience. In an age of hype and subterfuge, never underestimate the value of empathy, of shared feelings that somehow bring us inside one another. In his popular book, *The Road Less Travelled*, Scott Peck wrote: 'It is impossible to truly understand another without making room for that person within yourself.'

A friend can hear our words, see our joy or dry our tears, but to enter into our feelings is very different. We appreciate it when a friend goes beyond hearing what we are saying and clearly tries to feel our feelings of delight or depression. Hearing takes place easily in the ear, but feeling with another or them sharing our feelings is a deeper experience. These demand patient, generous caring, sustained, deliberate loving. We do not meet this often in our everyday encounters. 'I know how you feel' is easy to say. But to know and grasp for certain that a friend is even close to sharing our present feelings is an enriching and enjoyable experience. Joys are increased and sorrows lessened when a friend is genuinely trying to join us at this level.

There is much talk today of people-skills for management. This is often equated with the promotional stratagems of advertisers who are influencing us to part with our money. However, we know that real people-skill is built on a level of credibility and caring which leads people to share one another's values and feelings freely. Today it is more important than ever that we value the authenticity and sincerity of friendships in which we can share our emotional ups and downs. Real people-skill consists in having this willingness, together with the ability to identify with and to respond caringly to the feelings, moods, motives and needs of others.

Authentic human communication – as distinct from functional language like advertising or social noise taking place in an elevator – depends very much on people's ability to share their feelings. Communication that lacks some degree of mutual feeling is close to using one another – or at least it is flying blind around true friendship no matter how strong the handshake or tight the embrace. Abraham Lincoln is credited with this worthy thought: 'I don't like that man; I must get to know him better'. Undisciplined feelings can blind us, but the love in disciplined feelings enables us to see more. We see only what we love. If people are capable of loving, the revelation of weakness and vulnerability makes love grow.

Weddings and funerals are usually feeling-occasions. 'You look beautiful' or 'That is a lovely suit' are appreciated comments. So too are 'I am sorry for your loss' or 'I know you'll miss her so much'. Very often, something deeper can be communicated to a bride or bridegroom with a warm hug or a strong handshake without any words. The caring or joyful tears of those attending either a wedding or a funeral can express something richer. Usually, the sincere tears of our friends tell us that they do feel with us. Body language is often a deeper form of communication than words, and gestures can make words unnecessary when words are inappropriate. Observed body language is usually the first contact because it indicates feelings before any physical contact is made or before words are spoken.

Putting a name on the feelings of another can sometimes be done by a skilled counsellor or by an observant other, but to feel caringly with another and to let them know that we share their feelings is not easy. It is a precious experience. It is the deepest level of communication because heart is speaking to heart at that moment. It may not be expressed in words, and in fact it is often best expressed in body language. Relationships can begin by doing things together, but they grow only by seeing things together and in the sharing of each other's feelings. Feelings are the shortest distance between two people. When we permit people to share our feelings, we give them the privilege of possessing part of us because we know that they love us.

Before we can share in the feelings of another we must quieten our own thoughts and our own internal noise. It means deciding to forget our own concerns for some time. It is easier if the other person is already a friend, and wants us to share their feelings. It is difficult when the other person seems to resist. In either case, this sharing of another's feelings can leave us feeling drained, even exhausted. It helps to remember that the difficult person might only be a pleasant person who is just having a bad day. In many cases we have to – as it were – respectfully nibble our way under the other person's defensive, self-concealing conversation.

Occasionally we hear it said, 'But he does not communicate'. This is never true. When two people are together it is impossible not to communicate. Some communication always takes place, either in words, through eyes, by gesture or by silence. On occasion, one has to interpret the other's silence rather than their words. If I cannot hear their silence, I will not hear their words. Unless people are long-term friends, this attempt to feel with another person the journey into his or her inner experience generally calls for much patience, born of loving concern for the other.

It is so easy to hesitate or to give up trying to feel with people who are constantly unpleasant on the surface. The word *prejudice* means the act of pre-judging someone without taking the trouble to find all the facts. This incomplete information enables us to reach a conclusion about another person without looking at the whole person with their genetic history, their developmental history and their present state. When we receive a rejecting word or a push-off in any form from another, it can really be a cry from that person to be heard, to be felt-with, an expression of deep need. At any time, the mutual disclosure of vulnerability is one of the best ways to begin and to develop a deep friendship.

Unless the other person is willing, there is no way to enter fruitfully into their feelings. A strong lock, possessed only by each individual, guards privacy about feelings. It is only a message of caring, offered clearly, that will be given gradual access to this private world. I must be sure that you care before I let you know the vulnerability of my feelings. It is not difficult to see my activities, and it may not be difficult to know what I think. Generally, you can make an intelligent judgement about my values. But you can only guess at what I feel at any moment. For you to touch and to handle the world of my feelings, I must be sure that you have gentle, caring hands, and that you will listen with an open, non-judgemental mind and a big heart. You may have to go beyond my smiling defensiveness, or even endure my bad manners to achieve this.

In our desire to help another, we are all inclined to act as quickly as possible. This sincere attitude can be inspired by concern at the other's stress, without pausing long enough to discover just what the stress is, or how it is being felt. This reaction could happen when we try to equate the other's stress with a similar external circumstance in our own lives. This is the 'If I were you...' approach, which forgets that I was never and can never be you, or ever feel as you do, even in similar circumstances. It could be an attempt to solve a problem without understanding it fully. We may be trying to fix something before we find it. It is always good advice to hear me before you try to help me. This is where love expresses itself in patience and gentleness, leading to deeper listening.

Of course, it is ideal if one is fully aware of our own general feeling-repertoire or of our feeling at any given moment. It is only when we can turn down our own mental concerns or emotional state to a level of quietness that we can hope to feel with the other person at the feeling level. Then, we can touch the other person where they are happy, distressed, anxious or

confused. This cannot be achieved by intelligence and effort
alone. Hearing happens in the head; feeling comes from the
concerned heart. Reaching this level of intimacy occurs only
when we listen deeply enough to go below the surface of the
other person's social façade. As the poet Theodore Roethke
wrote, 'I've recovered my tenderness by long looking'.

CHAPTER SIX

# *To Love Is to Accept*

M OST of us have heard someone say to us, perhaps in a moment of impatience, 'If only you would change...' The words could have come carelessly from a close but weary friend or from someone who did not care about us very much. They could have been lovingly spoken for our benefit or for the benefit of the other. Either way, it is generally not a helpful remark when we know that either we cannot make the suggested change or make it at this time. When someone, however sincerely, is trying to push or pressure us to change, it can be quite stressful. We all like to be accepted as we are just now, even if we see the need to change and are willing to change later. We need the space to change without condemnation, criticism or manipulation by another. To change our learned behaviour is generally difficult, but to change our attitudes is much more demanding, especially as we age. It is only when we are loved and accepted as we are that we can listen to the invitation to change. This is important.

It is rather like the tourist who was lost at a certain spot and asked a passer-by the way, only to be told, 'If I were you I would not start from here at all.' The frustration which would come from hearing this foolish suggestion is clear. To move anywhere or to make any change in attitude or in behaviour, we can only start from the present situation or experience. It is never helpful to hear an invitation to begin change, without awareness and acceptance of the present position.

To be told that we would be more acceptable, more successful or happier if we were more intelligent, more beautiful or more handsome, or if we had more money, is frustrating and fruitless when the suggestion to change is impossible to fulfil. Even when a suggestion is possible to accept, but only partially, the 'If only you would...' approach, is equally pointless and sometimes quite cruel. It can sound like, or actually be a statement of rejection: 'I will accept you only if you change'. The statement can also often have the effect of making us feel guilty or inadequate. It is worth stressing that our friends may not remember what we said but they will remember how we made them feel. Our present experience, with all its strengths and limitations, could be described as 'where I am' or 'where I am at just now'. My present experience, my strengths and my weaknesses, are all part of me. I may change later, but they are who I am at this time. To reject my feelings is to reject me, and so deny the real me an opportunity to move forward from how I am at this time. Once I am told that I will be accepted when I alter my attitudes or behaviour, I am no longer accepted for who I am now. The speaker is accepting another person, and that person is me, but only if I change.

In his book *No Man is an Island*, monk and mystic Thomas Merton says:

> The beginning of love is the will to let those we love be perfectly themselves, not to twist them to fit our own image. If we do not accept them as they are, but only their potential likeness to ourselves, then we do not love them; we only love the reflection of ourselves that we find in them.

Genuine hospitality is freely to accept another person into our home or into our heart. This type of hospitality is easy with people who share our views and our feelings, but to offer hospitality to another when they do not deserve it is more demanding. All major religions recommend some kind of hospitality towards the lost, the lonely, the foreigner, the homeless, the migrant and the stranger. True hospitality does not come with a demand to change, even if the host hopes for some change in the guest. The open door or open-heart does not have the sign, 'Enter if…', or 'provided that'. This would be hospitality with conditions attached, hospitality with a hyphen.

Even a sincere willingness to lovingly accept another 'where they are at' could be misinterpreted. Some people have been so rejected early in life that they turn away from genuine acceptance by another, or experience a sense of rejection where it is not intended. This response is to be regretted, but we know that perception is reality for the person perceiving. It is a situation that calls for much patience and one that will test the authenticity of the other's love. To love someone is to look deeply, to understand and often to wait patiently until the other person begins to feel accepted.

To accept someone where they are *at* is not the same as to accept them as they are. If parents accept their children as they are, the children will never grow to maturity. Parents must always remain lovingly restless for a child's growth. This approach requires parents to always accept the child-at-age, and be satisfied with the behaviour appropriate to a child at its present stage of development; this is where the child is *at*. Otherwise the child will develop a feeling of being rejected, because the parents' expectations are too high, too demanding or not in keeping with the child's age and with what can be expected at that stage of development. This parent-child example applies to every human interaction. Before inviting a person to develop or helping them to do so, one must fully accept them where they are *at*.

After a willingness to feel with the other, this is the second stage in loving. True love allows other people the freedom to *be*, and gives them the invitation to change when necessary, without condemnation, criticism or manipulation.

True love is not blind; in fact, it sees more. It does not close its eyes to the weaknesses of the other but it opens its eyes more widely and sees more deeply into the potential and possibilities for growth in the one loved. True love refuses to be blinded by bad manners, by apparent rejection, by abiding fears or by the hesitant insecurities which come from the other. Love persists in seeing below the surface. It is for this reason that a person, however flawed, who is accepted by one other, never feels alone, never feels without hope. That too is why the first step in loving is to feel with the whole of the other person, and not just in relation to their unpleasant qualities. Authentic love is ready to find explanations and excuses for the other's failures to measure up. It is willing to encourage the other's growth and to await their development of more pleasant qualities. True love is confident that it is only by loving acceptance that some change may occur. And so, love waits patiently.

Often enough people can benefit from direct advice or from correction, but these efforts are usually more successful when they feel that the person trying to help accepts them as they are. When this does not happen, the results make disturbing reading.

A few years ago, a priest in his mid-forties came to me for counselling. At the end of the first interview I offered him diagnostic testing in order to discover the underlying dynamic of his personality. He agreed. His results confirmed what he had already suspected, that he was significantly homosexually oriented. It also showed that he was suffering from a serious obsessive-compulsive syndrome. This state is always accompanied by severe anxiety. While confirming the test result, he said that he had been more than usually anxious since his childhood.

His parents were people of deep faith and regular religious practice but rather narrow in their beliefs. Even in primary school he felt that he was somehow different from his classmates, but he lived with the discomfort because he was unable to describe the feeling that he was unaccepted. Early in secondary school, when he heard his friends talk about girls and about sexuality, he was able to recognize his lack of sexual interest in girls. At that time, homosexuality was not spoken about openly, or it was referred to derisively. As a result of this mind-set, he had great difficulty in accepting his orientation, even in his mind and feelings.

Eventually he spoke to his mother who brushed his problem aside; she could not accept it. When he turned to his father, the only response he received was to be told that his difficulties would pass. He joined his wife in her inability to accept their son's gayness even when the boy made frequent attempts to be heard and accepted. He approached a priest who could not help him beyond assuring him that his orientation was not sinful. At university, the female chaplain advised him to date a few girls. He said that he got on well with the girls but that he felt no sexual attraction towards any of them. Gradually, the girls did not respond to his invitations. His anxiety, his loneliness and his compulsive tendencies increased.

At the age of 20 he felt a call to become a priest and he was enthusiastically encouraged by his mother. In the seminary he settled well for a short time into the all-male environment. However, he soon felt a sexual attraction towards another seminarian who indicated a similar feeling towards him. Encouraged by his spiritual director, he succeeded in avoiding physical contact with his fellow seminarian, but this strain increased his stressful anxiety. During his holidays, he brought the matter up with his mother, who was the more dominant person in his home, but she still could not accept how he felt.

During his final years in the seminary, Church leaders directed that, when a homosexual orientation was 'deep seated', the person should not be accepted into a seminary. Then another directive came from Rome to say that the homosexual condition was 'intrinsically disordered'. Although his spiritual guide told him not to pay attention to these instructions, he felt even more unaccepted by the entire Church. Although the difference was explained to him by a priest, he said that he was unable to accept that his entire personhood was not 'intrinsically disordered'. His non-acceptance by his mother and then by the Church spread to an inability to accept himself.

Two years after his ordination he left the priesthood. He is now sharing his life harmoniously with a male partner. His obsessive tendencies and his anxieties have decreased but have not gone away. He still suffers from his parents' failure to accept him.

This story shows us the importance of acceptance. Someone truly loves us when he or she brings us home to ourselves, when they help us to be comfortable with who we are and who we can become. Home is not just a place; it is a feeling which depends on how much we are able to be at peace with ourselves and accepted by our loved ones. It has less to do with geography *where* we are than it has to do with being surrounded by people who accept us *as* we are, and who encourage us into a future where we can grow to be our best selves.

# CHAPTER SEVEN

# *To Love Is to Encourage*

THE DECISION to love another always leads us to a desire that the loved one becomes his or her best self. No loving friend is happy to see the other stagnate in their physical, mental, emotional or spiritual development. Those who love us often see greater possibilities within us than we ourselves see. Every person is unfinished growth; and while we may resist it, all of us appreciate a gentle, friendly invitation to move forward and to complete that growth towards being our uniquely best selves.

One can resist or shrug off invitations to grow. There are social forces today which press for passivity and conformity and tempt people to remain satisfied with where they are and to plateau out in their personal improvement. In addition, many people are so busy with financial survival that they have become tired and tend to neglect deep care for themselves. Many are tired or close to exhaustion as they seek employment or anxiously try to hold on to their present job or search for promotion. Thoughts and plans for personal growth are not foremost in their minds. People in these stressful situations tend to forget or to resist any invitation to care more for themselves and to grow. They tend to neglect or resist invitations to nurture their own growth.

Time is like a washing machine; it can shrink our ideals. At some stage in our lives, we are all tempted to languish lazily with half-evolved talents. We talk about starting something desirable or about giving up something undesirable, but our actions often carry a lot of 'wait'. Words continue to be firm, but perseverance becomes flabby. Sometimes we all need a kick in the seat of our '*can'ts*'. If we love a friend, it pains us to see them in need of this invitation to grow towards their own best selves, or away from persevering in some form of self-harm. Everyone needs a friend to challenge them quietly. We need someone to call us out of our comfort zones, and help us to leave them. To love another is to invite him or her to make progress; to care is to call them forward.

Lest we get discouraged in loving our friends enough to move forward in this way, it is worth remembering that, despite apparent or real resistance, deep down everyone desires to grow. When we love someone, we feel called to touch and to trigger off that desire in them. Loving means that we try to remind those whom we love that there is something within them that is superior to circumstances. When we encourage friends, we help them to believe that the power within them is greater than the pressure around them. Sigmund Freud said that while we are products of the past, we are not prisoners of the past. He also said that each of us is not only worse than we think, we are also better than we think we are. There are unexplored areas and untested limits within all our friends, and, perhaps even without being aware of it, they await our encouraging touch in order to explore these areas and to stretch these unexplored limits.

There is only one freedom that we cannot comfortably give to someone we love, and that is the freedom not to grow. True friends always desire their friends to grow. To give a friend the false freedom to stagnate is to love them less, somehow to betray them. It is to fail to visit them deeply and to invite them out of their prison of stunted growth. Yet, we cannot demand or in any way force this growth which can only be loved into life.

An invitation to change, no matter how gently it is given, can risk offending the other. It can be interpreted as interference or as an attempt to manipulate. Our intentions may be selfless, but so much depends on how the person we love is able to receive our invitation. It is often useful to ask ourselves why we want our friend to change. Is it entirely for their good or is it partially for our own benefit? Most people are quick to sense if it is for the latter, and they rightfully resist what can accurately be called manipulation. Should we find our motives to be selfish, it is wise to find a more selfless person to help that person. Everything depends on how much our friend feels we have accepted him or her (as explained in the last chapter). However, as delicate as this way of helping another is, the *Book of Proverbs* encourages us: 'Reprove a wise man and he will love you; give him instruction and he will grow in wisdom'. (*Proverbs* 9:8)

Much interpersonal communication is little more than social noise as we pass one another in a hurry. In order to live and work together, much communication is functional: its purpose is to get things done with reasonable harmony. However, when we have deep interpersonal communication aimed at communion, we influence one another, and we each have power that gently encourages the other to listen more deeply and to act in new ways. We can achieve this change by our words or by our example.

This power could be called *authority* in its deepest meaning. Authority has the same root as the word *author (auctor* in Latin). We can each be an author, a source of the other's growth towards more life. We all have this kind of authority over friends who respect us, and especially over intimate friends. While selfish power says 'go', good authority says 'come'. Power pushes; authority proposes. Power inveigles, but good authority invites. When selfish power is used over another person it is usually for some purpose outside of themselves, but when selfless authority is used, it is always for the other's well-being and growth. Power often lacks patience and it sometimes punishes, while authority accepts that all growth is gradual and partial. Perhaps that is why some people in leadership positions today have to rely on the use of raw power. They lack the authenticity of a selfless love.

In our desire and efforts to change people, even for their own good, the temptation to use power or pressure is never far away. In his book *The Will to Power*, Karl Jung wrote: 'Power not only corrupts, but it raises rival structures of unfreedom and aggression. Where love rules, there is no will to power, but where power predominates, there love is lacking.' One is the shadow-opposite of the other. The captain of a Roman legion left this inscription carved on a small monument in North Africa: 'I, the captain of a Legion of Rome, have learnt and pondered this truth, that there are two things in life, love and power, and no man can exercise both.'

There are many occasions when we cannot help someone in a way that brings obvious results. But it is a rare day when we cannot gently invite another person to grow more away from what may be harmful to them or slowing down their personal growth. Consider the word *present*. Two objects are *present near* each other. Two animals are *present with* each other. Two people who have no relationship can be *present to* each without any love passing between them. Only people who love and care for one another are *present for* each other. This presence *for* the other is often explicit and demonstrably clearm particularly when we praise our friend's effort or their goodness or their success. More often the presence *for* the other is communicated subconsciously and with equal clarity in a smile or hug. One of the most helpful ways to encourage others is to describe our own struggles.

Italian novelist, Primo Levi, in his book *If This Is a Man*, describing his survival in Auschwitz death camp, wrote:

> I believe that it was really due to Lorenzo that I am alive today; and not so much for his physical help, as by his presence, by his natural and plain manner of being good. He reminded me that there still exists a world outside our own, something and someone still pure and not corrupt, not savage. It is something difficult to define, a remote possibility of good, but for which it was worth surviving.

The old phrase, 'giving good example' can have very deep meaning.

Pierre Teilhard de Chardin wrote to a friend: 'We are one after all, you and I. Together we exist. Together we suffer. Together we struggle, and forever will re-create each other'. Florence Nightingale seemed to stress the same duty and privilege to create one another when she wrote: 'I think that God said to us, create the world.' By loving encouragement, we continue to create one another.

Even those who are unfriendly, or whom we regard as enemies, can encourage us without intending to do so. Edmund Burke, the great Irish orator in the English parliament, wrote: 'Everyone needs an enemy. He who wrestles with us strengthens our moral fibre and sharpens our skill. Our antagonist is our helper, but I need to believe that my antagonist may be right.' Saying almost the same thing, the German philosopher Karl Jaspers said: 'Loving combat is the deepest form of communication'. Thomas Berry wrote: 'It is only in an engaged life with our enemy that we discover who we are, what creativity is and what our destiny is'. Real friends can disagree, discuss and even dispute at an effective level.

A psychology professor in New Delhi told me of an experiment that he conducted to discover the value of encouragement. Among his students was one girl who was not pretty, less tall than average, somewhat overweight, and possessing a low self-image. The professor asked three of his male students to pay constant attention to the girl, and to ask her for regular dates for a period of six months. After five months, he noticed that the girl had grown in self-confidence, lost weight and dressed more attractively than before. Part of the professor's plan was that the three young men would tell her about the experiment after six months. He predicted that, on being told of the experiment, she would return to her low self-image, even though he hoped that this would not happen. In fact, the girl did not revert to her previous, low self-image. The girl built up her feeling of self-worth and kept it, even enabling her to thank the three male fellow-students, and later to marry another man of her choice. Nothing is so important or so loving as to help another person to strengthen their feeling of self-worth and to hear their own music, the music of their best selves coming from within.

Sometimes one word or one sentence helps to encourage, for the simple reason that even one friendly word recognises our existence. I have found that any transaction, even across a counter, can be a silent impersonal exchange or it can be enriched by a human remark like 'You are very busy today', or 'It's nearly your time to go home', or 'Thanks for your smile'. Simple eye contact, and especially a smile, can enhance any contact between two people. Unless a street is very busy, a simple 'Hello' can encourage.

# CHAPTER EIGHT

# To Love Is to Help

WHEN we have discovered a real need within another person, and when we have encouraged them to want to grow, our next step is often to do something for them, to help them in whatever way we can. This approach is always the human, loving and noble thing to do. I recall that my grandfather often said to me that being helpful to unkind people is especially important because they need it most.

Most of us wish to help our close friends in their troubles and to assist them in prospering or in developing in the way they need. We wish to help friends towards full physical health, good emotional balance, mental efficiency and spiritual harmony when this help is needed. However, in practice, the best way to help these people is often difficult to initiate. That is why it is rarely a good idea to start helping too quickly unless the need is urgent and obvious. It is better to pause, listen and think about what is the real need of the one we love. Feeling with the other, listening deeply to them and encouraging them to grow must come before helping them.

At other times, we can help people easily and directly, as when they need a loan or some material help. At other times, finding the best way to help is more difficult. Generally, it is better to help people to help themselves, unless they are incapable of doing so. As noted in an earlier chapter, it is important to discover what will really help the other person, to find where their deepest real need is. This means more than just hearing the words they are using. By listening deeply, by feeling with them, we can discover best what help they need, and how to give it. In his autobiography, Danish philosopher Søren Kierkegaard reminds us:

> In order to help another effectively, I must understand what he understands. If I do not know that, my greatest understanding will be of no help to him … Instruction begins when you put yourself in his place, so that you may understand what he understands and in the way he understands it.

One can give help without loving, but one cannot truly love without helping. This often begins by painstakingly trying to discover the best way to help the other. For instance, to give money to a compulsive gambler, or whiskey to an alcoholic, eases their frustration momentarily, but it is not helping them. Giving a child or an adolescent access to some TV programmes can be very harmful to them. Giving a book or an article to someone could be very helpful, provided we know that this particular item will help their deepest need. Giving advice is often helpful, but people wise enough to give advice are usually sensible enough to give it sparingly or not at all. Silent caring company is often better than big doses of well-intentioned advice.

There is always a danger that we are responding to our own needs, rather than to the needs of the person we love. This level of understanding can easily develop into a situation called co-dependency, where both people become locked into an addictive situation of satisfying their individual needs compulsively – one giving and the other receiving. Our love and willingness to help must have the other's deeper and long-term welfare in mind, rather than an apparent immediate need as either perceives it to be. In other words, all loving help must be given at the point of the other's authentic long-term need. Occasionally, it may be that someone else can give more beneficial help than we can at any particular time, and true love is usually humble enough to recognize this likelihood.

When another person knows that we care about them, that we have an attitude which tells them from our face or gestures of our willingness to give them time, or that we deeply desire their welfare, we are helping them without doing anything. When the loved one knows that we are, so to speak, caringly on their side, always present for them even when we are absent, this awareness helps them. When we are unable to support someone by changing a sad or stressful situation, as when their close relative dies, then a silent touch or a few tears or a tight handshake will be really helpful A brief phone call, flowers or a card sent can say so much, provided that a loving attitude is already known to be present.

When we are present near people, our body language is always giving a message, whether we know it or not. Day-to-day interaction between people in the home, at work or at play can carry a message of caring love in some measure and at different levels. However, there are always limits to how far we can help in most situations. These limits depend on the quality of the relationship or perhaps on the time available. Ideally we can say that we love everyone equally and all the time, but the limits of our energy, our availability, our finance, our closeness to and our contact with them clearly limit any expression of our love in helping others. Each of us has one lifetime, only 24 hours in each day, money that is limited, and energy that flags. With all our heart we can love our spouses, the poor and trafficked slaves or the starving people in a poor country, in the sense that we deeply wish them all well, but we cannot help them all equally, due to the limits of being human.

Real love has no limits to its depth, but it has real limits in how often and how deeply we can express it. The only mistake is to do nothing when you can do only a little.

Unquestionably, the best form of help is to build up another person's self-image, to increase their feeling of self-worth. This support gives them confidence to survive under stress, and helps them to deal with the challenges of life. In Pakistan, where brides are sometimes paid for, a father of five daughters told me how a suitor came to his home and before choosing his future bride, asked to meet all five. There was a different price on each of them, depending on their looks and skills. He was told that he could have the least good-looking, almost illiterate and rather shy girl in exchange for one cow. Something in him made her attractive to him and he offered two cows for her. After their marriage, and on hearing him say what he thought she was worth, she turned out to be a wonderfully loving and outgoing person. This was because he had built up her feeling of self-worth. Everything we do to build up another person's self-regarding sentiment helps them more than anything we can give them.

Our thoughts expressed in words can help when we assist a person to see something beautiful in themselves that they did not previously recognize, or perhaps to see a strength or weakness in a different way. The mind or heart stretched to a new idea never reverts to its original dimensions. When people are stressed, they tend to become a little blind or to use tunnel thinking which limits them in their search for solutions; they can easily fail to see possibilities; and often it takes only a few words to alert them to a way out of the stress or to find a better solution. That is why even a thought offered for consideration can be a real help. 'Have you ever considered this...?' can be a very helpful phrase.

However, thoughts and words can also be very easy ways to avoid helping. As we sometimes say, words are cheap. That is why giving advice might even be considered a last resort. Giving advice presumes that we have every aspect of the situation and every detail of the other person's experience clearly in our heads. And this is rarely so. It is tantamount to using the useless phrase, 'If I were you...', as explained above.

We can, of course, try to help people we love when we are sure they are travelling a harmful path like alcoholism or drug addiction. This attempt, however, is always a risk, as it depends on how close we are to the person we are trying to help. Correction usually arouses defensiveness and, in some cases, even aggression. Nobel-winning psychologist Daniel Kahneman, in his book *Thinking Fast and Slow,* has shown that humans have a tendency to steer clear of facts that would force their brains to work harder. In some cases, it was found that confronting people – however lovingly – with correcting facts even strengthens their unwise behaviour. This outcome is called 'the backfire effect'. But when the relationship is deep, help is usually accepted even if it takes some time. Careful wording of the helpful correction is of prime importance, even among friends. The gentler approach of concerned questions is usually better than direct advice.

The example of our own life, as seen by others, can be a great help even when no words are spoken. This is particularly true when the loved one in need sees a somewhat similar successful struggle having taken, or taking place. As noted earlier, disclosing our own vulnerability and our own efforts helps others greatly. People may be able to identify with both our weaknesses and our frustrations in the struggle.

On one occasion, on a very crowded street in Dakka, Bangladesh, I saw two old men arm-in-arm struggling through the dense crowd. My companion, another priest, approached them with some money. He discovered that one of them was blind, and the other lame. He pointed out to me that, if alone, both of them would be helpless, but that together they were managing well enough with their handicaps. It surely must have been a great moment when they first met to begin a life of helping each other with their shared disabilities. Or should we thank the person who introduced them? To reveal and share weaknesses is always a mutually helpful experience. This quote from St Augustine is apposite:

> Where we are equally confident, let my listener strive on with me. Where we are equally puzzled, let him pause to investigate with me. Where he finds me in error, let him come to my side, and where he finds me hesitant let him call me to his side.

Despite his international reputation in music and theology, Albert Schweitzer became a doctor and gave his life to the poor of French Equatorial Africa. He wrote this to a friend: 'I do not know what your destiny will be, but one thing I do know: the only ones among us who will be truly happy are those who will have sought and have found how to serve'.

True love is a willingness to help another person by example, by inspiration, by a smile or simple word, by a gift or, perhaps, by a hand on the shoulder. Because love always enriches the loved one, any loving act goes on for ever. Kind words and deeds are eternal; we never know where they end. If in doubt, always do the loving thing by listening first, by accepting what we find, and by helping where we can. The French philosopher

Voltaire wrote, 'Every man is guilty of the good he did not do'. And in the *Talmud*, which is the spiritual centre of Jewish life, we read: 'Seeing an act of kindness, God says that for that moment alone it was worth creating the world'. Remember, that if all that can be said of us in the end, is that we were always helpful, that is enough.

# CHAPTER NINE

# *To Love Is to Forgive*

THERE IS no communication or interaction between friends, acquaintances or strangers that does not at some time result in occasional annoyances and hurts. Life presents us with endless occasions when we need to be forgiven and to forgive. Forgiveness is part of life and of loving. Some hurtful moments can be caused deliberately, but most of them are not intended. However, intended or not, and unless we become hermits, getting hurt and feeling the need to forgive are inescapable.

Constantly repeated decisions to forgive can be exhausting. For this reason, it is more ideal that forgiveness becomes an attitude, a readiness – not always instant – to pardon or to overlook. This attitude will make individual acts of forgiveness much easier. Growth in this readiness to forgive begins with a decision to cultivate it and to practise it as often as possible. Repeated actions will gradually form an attitude. This remains true even when the actions are difficult to perform. Susan Jeffers gives us good advice in the title of her book, *Feel the Fear and Do It Anyway*. A forgiving attitude grows by acting contrary to negative feelings. It is developed slowly, and even after having achieved this inclination to forgive, it is still possible to fail occasionally. However, as we develop a forgiving attitude, we become more able to deflect words or actions that might otherwise stay within our subconscious.

Central to developing a forgiving attitude is to realize that feelings do not forgive. The best we can hope for from hurt feelings is that they will gradually fade unless we keep recalling them. When a nasty word is spoken, and when a hurtful deed is done to us, or when we are let down, it is our feelings that react immediately. We may reflect on it later, or we may use words to describe it, but the hurt remains in our feelings. It is in our feelings that we experience the pain, and all feelings have a separate existence from our thoughts and desires. No matter how we may forgive a blow on the nose, the initial hurt feeling can remain with us. Forgiveness is not a feeling; like all loving, it is a choice, a decision. Both pleasant and unpleasant feelings have a very strong memory, because they are embedded deeply within us, and it takes time for them to subside or to disappear. They came uninvited, and they cannot be invited to go. So, it is important not to expect forgiveness in the feelings which remain after a hurt. Feelings do not forgive.

We can experience our feelings, and we can reflect on them, but we cannot command them to change. While we cannot dictate to our feelings, we can train them to have less power over us. By looking sympathetically at human weakness in others, we are less inclined to cling to hurts received. Given time, we may be able to develop a fairly permanent forgiving stance. Most unkind words or deeds have their deeper origin in unconscious hurt, simmering perhaps since childhood. The word compassion comes from two Latin words, *cum* ('with') and *patiar / passus* ('to suffer'). When we can recognize the pain that lies beneath the unkind deed of the other, we can suffer with them rather than condemn them. That is compassion.

We can talk with our feelings but we cannot talk at them. Talking about positive or negative ones can increase them. Replaying joyful feelings is always a good idea. Deliberately looking back at negative feelings is unwise and unhelpful. If we do so, we can end up with an enduring feeling that most people are against us. When we do not forgive, the person who hurt us has taken possession of part of us, leaving us less than a fully free person. By not forgetting the past, we are also carrying the burden of the past in the limited space of our memories. Taking revenge, or wishing to get even, diminishes us, shrinks us. Eventually we run the serious risk of living with constant hypersensitivity, of moving from being a victim to living in a miserable state of victimhood. This outlook can be the beginning of a paranoid personality disorder, leading to a permanent delusion of being persecuted. It can end up by limiting our trust in everyone.

There are many reasons why it is not healthy to remain in a state of unforgiveness which gnaws at the inside of the resentful one. When we hold on to this attitude, like acid, it eats away at our peace of mind. Occasional conscious recall of a hurt is to be expected, but it can be managed unless we continue to recall it and perhaps indulge in it. As long as we keep a person down, some part of us has to be down there holding them. I once asked a woman if she actually hated the man who had been unfaithful to her. Her reply was: 'No one will ever drag me down so low.' If you take revenge you may believe that you have 'got even', but when you forgive, you have become superior. Forgiveness is to be in control.

Unwillingness to forgive can express itself in very obvious ways, such as a refusal to meet with or talk to the person whom we consider to have been unjust to us. It can also live on and show itself in more subtle ways: for example, we can be sullen or give the other person the silent treatment in what is often called 'picture but no sound'. To spend a few moments like this is understandable or acceptable among real friends, but to prolong this stance hurts both the offender and the offended.

If we live with the one who hurt us, unforgiveness can tempt us to continue saying 'You always do that' or 'There you are again...' or 'I told you before...' or 'You should have...'. Harping on about the other's failure after we have pointed it out, increases the hurt for both persons. Real hurt should be named to the person who caused it, but preferably at a later date, when both people are relaxed. At that stage, it is best to name the problem just once, not to keep repeating it. If the offensive words or behaviour have to be brought up, 'Next time perhaps we can...' is a much more productive beginning to a sentence than by using condemnatory phrases such as, 'You should not have...'

Not infrequently, people who love us hurt us without intending to do so or even when trying to be kind. A French proverb can be loosely translated: 'No action, however dutiful, is of more value than a mistake committed through tenderness' (*tout le devoir ne vaut pas une faute qui s'est comise par tendresse*). We can always try to assess what possible good intention may have been behind a word or deed which hurt us.

A forgiving attitude, a tendency to forgive, is more important than individual acts of forgiveness. A tendency to take offence leads to a frequent readiness to feel hurt. For this reason, it is helpful to realise that offence given does not have to be offence taken. As we develop a forgiving attitude we become more able to deflect words or actions which might otherwise sink into us and stay within us. Our readiness to forgive is often a test of our maturity; or, to put it simply, we are as big as the things which bother us.

There is a simple technique which enables us to remove, or at least lessen, negative feelings like resentment that we wish to be rid of. Sit alone and take deep breaths for a few moments, trying to be aware of the air entering and leaving through your nostrils. Then imagine what colour your negative feeling is and put a colour on it. As you breathe out, visualize, imagine that colour and blow it out energetically through your mouth. Then decide what colour you think relaxed peace might be, and put it on the air that you are breathing in. Feel free to choose any colour you wish for your negative and positive feelings of resentment and peace. Many people choose to put a black or a dark purple colour on their negative feelings and to put turquoise blue or yellow on their positive feelings; but it is best to make your own choice. While it is more helpful to sit quietly when you do this breathing exercise, you can practise it while you are walking. It is a useful exercise before you sleep, in keeping with Paul's advice to the Christians at Ephesus: 'Do not let the sun go down on your anger.'

When you have identified what it is in the other that upsets you, it is useful to ask yourself: Is this same trait or tendency in yourself, perhaps subconsciously? We call this projection, and it happens quite frequently. We dislike in others what we are inclined to hide in ourselves. To become aware of ourselves doing this, to name it and to claim it, is real progress.

We can forgive sincerely and deeply while still feeling very hurt. Deliberate unkind words or deeds can indeed hurt, and they inflict at least temporary damage on a relationship, especially if it is a close one. At the same time, friendships are often deepened by an act of forgiveness. If friendship can be compared with a silken thread between two people, and if hurtful words or actions can be described as a fraying of the thread, forgiveness can then be a strengthening of the thread by tying a knot over the frayed part. As more knots become necessary, the thread becomes shorter and friends grow closer. The poet Alfred Lord Tennyson describes this beautifully:

—

And blessing on the falling out
That all the more endears,
When we fall out with those we love
And kiss again in tears.

Here are some questions that can help to measure the sincerity and the level of forgiveness in any situation.

1. Do I refrain from wishing evil on the person who offended me?
2. Do I refrain from actually doing something to hurt the other person?
3. Do I refrain from speaking evil of that person?
4. Do I try not to dwell on the offence?
5. Do I refrain from speaking about the offending event again?
6. Do I greet the person when they do not initiate the greeting?
7. If the person who offended me asked for help, would I help?
8. Would I spontaneously offer help to the person if he or she were in need?
9. Would I ask the offending person to help me when I am in need?

Each of these levels is one step deeper in an increasing act of forgiveness, and each of them is a loving action no matter how we feel, even if we cannot get beyond the first one.

There can exist a situation when serious harm was done to someone, such as walking out of a marriage, physical injury inflicted, or a large amount of money stolen. Forgiveness may seem impossible. But if the seriously offended person wishes they could forgive, or however vaguely, hopes to forgive much later, we can say that forgiveness in some form is present. Deliberate serious hurt leaves deep injury that must often be given a long time to heal.

Finally, remember that forgiveness is to choose a future in freedom, rather than the one imposed by the slavery of re-membering a painful past. Forgiving love is always an enriching experience.

# CHAPTER TEN

# *To Love Is to Celebrate*

THE DICTIONARY says that we celebrate when we publicly acknowledge a significant or happy day with a social gathering or enjoyable activity. Another dictionary describes celebration as taking part in a special, enjoyable activity in order to show that a particular occasion is important.

Psychologists offer the following five stages in a relationship, as a guide for people growing together: inclusion, care, trust, affection and playfulness. This model is a framework for thinking about love between people, but it is also important to remember that all relationships are fluid, dynamic and partially unpredictable.

*Inclusion* is when one person offers an invitation to friendship, whether by eye contact, a smile, a friendly 'Hello' or a direct request. *Care* implies a genuine concern for the other's welfare and motivates us to further another person's needs and interests. *Trust* means that two people are sure they can safely predict that each of them will act consistently in being positive and constructive in their friendship. The next stage is *affection*, which is characterized by feelings of warmth and attachment, and is expressed in a desire to be close to the other. This affection is communicated in words or non-verbally by touch or by smiles, by glances and by tender looks. It is also manifested in authentic sexual intimacy. *Playfulness* is about celebrating together, enjoying each other's company. Relaxed body movement like dancing. A feeling of joy or laughter often accompany playfulness and celebration but can also be expressed through quiet relaxation in the other's company.

Why do people feel the need to celebrate? In the opening sentence in Scott Peck's book *The Road Less Travelled*, he states, 'Life is difficult'. In his later book *Further Along the Road*, he added, 'Life is complex'. We need to celebrate in order to escape, at least for a while, from the difficulties and complexities of life, for a chat with a friend, for an evening out, for a dance together or for a holiday.

I became very aware of this in the small and poorer villages of South America and in the southern Philippines. Often, despite their very limited wealth and few possessions, the people of every village held a few work-free days of fiesta, during which they ate, drank, sang and danced. I asked an older Filipina if, in view of their hard struggles, the fiesta was not a little extravagant or wasteful. With a tolerant smile, she said to me that there was not much fun in medicine, but that there is good medicine in fun. She reminded me that, during these days of festivity, they were able to forget their struggles and their hard lives, to which they returned perhaps tired but refreshed.

Most people's lives in developed countries are increasingly permeated by demanding work outside the home. This toil is added to the demands of raising a family and to domestic work in their homes. Paying a mortgage is another stress for many and periods of unemployment are more so. The breakdown of relationships or the illness of friends and of family members can make life very arduous. Loneliness is one of life's greatest burdens, and the speed of life today gives rise to much anxiety, because people seem to have less time and money to enjoy life together. All of these can make life very stressful or even exhausting. In many ways, life today is more demanding than in the past.

All of us need healthy moments of escape from life's pressures. When these moments are shared in some form of celebration, they become even more effective than if we are alone. Someone offered this very visual observation: 'When you keep your eye on the ball, your nose to the grindstone, your shoulder to the wheel and your back to the wall, see how long you can survive'.

On one occasion in Calcutta when I was unusually busy I hesitated to accept an invitation to go out for a meal. The sight of so many poor people around us added to my hesitation. A wise old priest pointed to an ant heap near us, and he reminded me that ants work very hard, but that they never miss a picnic. When I was younger and inclined to forget a weekly day off work, a doctor in Sydney said something I did not easily forget: 'Stop or you'll stop'. The Japanese have a word, *karochi*, which means, death from overwork. The relaxation of celebration is important in all our lives.

Enjoyment of beauty together seems to deepen the experience for persons who love each other. Notice that people rarely go to the theatre or visit an art gallery alone. Any shared activity, from going for a walk together to spending a few hours in another's company revisiting places of cherished memories are enriching forms of celebration. We witness a very down-to-earth celebration as people come together in the local pub in the evening. Everything from having a cup of tea together to dressing up for a meal out with a friend can express and build up love. A holiday with a difficult person whom you are trying to love could be too much, but with a friend it can be real relaxation, real celebration. Working together on a common project, such as improving each other's home, brings people together, and doing some voluntary work with pleasant people also enhances relationships enjoyably.

It has been noted that while humans have much in common with animals, only humans have the capacity to continue playfulness and celebration into adulthood. Only humans are glad to invite their children back home when they have grown up; animals do not. The psychology of Transactional Analysis has a name for this important aspect of human growth: it is called 'exercising our adult childhood'. This behaviour occurs when adults choose to play rather like children, but without childishness; and it is always a good sign of maturity or of adulthood when a person has the capacity for shared enjoyment. Doing the same things alone can be personally rewarding, and at times it is necessary for real relaxation; but when enjoyment is shared, individuals not only benefit themselves, but it is also a time when one enriches the other.

Any celebration among friends is easily experienced as enriching. Perhaps less obviously enriching is a selfless decision to invite someone who is not pleasant company to spend some time with us. Because there is a clear element of unselfishness in this decision, it is very authentic loving. When it is less pleasant or less enjoyable for us to freely telephone, write to, visit, or go out with another person, we can be sure that we are loving. Quite often, when we persevere patiently and generously in this practice, we begin to see the other person as more lovable, and we are able to move from mild dislike of them to compassion for their limitations.

We should never underestimate the ability of genuine loving to make another person more human and more attractive. These people may not be close friends, and we may not be able to change their sadness or loneliness by our words. But our willingness to give them some of our time can build them up. While they may forget everything we said to them, they will remember how we made them feel and perhaps they may then hesitatingly begin to celebrate with us and within their lonely selves. At times when someone is depressed or feeling lonely, an invitation to celebrate in any way enriches both participants.

When distance makes celebration together impossible, letter writing or contact through email can be a valuable expression of celebration. Nowadays we have telephones in our pockets, enabling us to send a celebratory 'Hello' or to share good news with friends. Using Skype enables us to have virtual physical presence, even at great distances. Many of us have found that, on quite a few occasions, our call came just at the time when our friend needed it most. The result – a moment of love and celebration together.

Silence with a close friend can also be a time of love expressed and of celebration. Silence is one of the great arts of conversation, and many have lost it. A Japanese Shinto monk once said to me that there is no noise when a lilac bush speaks to us as its blossoms appear, or when the sky leaks with starlight or when snow pads the city with inches of silent beauty or when a spring morning offers itself for divine inspection. The Buddha wrote: 'Learn this from the waters. In the mountain clefts and chasms, the streamlets gush loudly, but deep rivers flow silently'. Caring silence can be more lifegiving than any loudly given advice, and in healthy relationships the quieter two people become the more they hear each other. In the year 6 BC the Chinese sage Lao Tzu said: 'The greatest revelation is celebration in stillness', echoed in the words of the Indian philosopher Bara Ram Dass: 'The quieter you become, the more you hear'. When there is love between two people, they can hear it best in loving silence. Parents sitting quietly with each other in silence are celebrating more deeply than their sons and daughters at a disco.

Sadly, it is true that some people suffer from an illness called *anhedonia*, which manifests itself in a lack of ability to enjoy pleasure, especially in social relationships and in recreational activities with others. They cannot engage in the important activity of celebration with those who love them. Most of these people can be helped gradually by someone who continues to reach out to them with love and patience despite their occasional refusal to respond. Their shell can be gently prised open by a telephone call or by inviting them to a shared meal, maybe under the pardonable pretence that we need a little boost ourselves. Simple gestures like these can lead to success and celebration.

Eric Fromm stated that the use of the body for the purpose of expressing satisfaction and celebration with one another is what sex truly is and what gives it its deepest meaning. For him, sex is important not only in its role of initial attraction and procreation but also in the bonding of a loving relationship through the fulfilment and pleasure it offers.

A few years ago I was ministering to a dying mother who was surrounded by her ten adult children. They were reciting a long repetitive prayer aloud. I suggested that they cease for a moment, and I asked them if their mother had had a great life which they enjoyed with her. They all agreed that this was so. I asked them if they thought we should celebrate it, and again they agreed, so we sang her favourite hymn and finished with three Alleluias ('May God be praised') in celebration of their mother's loving life. This brought a gentle smile to their mother's face and tears to all our eyes. When I met them afterwards, they thanked me for that unique moment celebrating a beautiful life. There is an inevitable sadness when friends die but there are also many delightful memories of love to celebrate.

The celebration of life begins when I accept the giftedness

of myself and begin to hear my own music. When I feel loved, it is important to celebrate it alone or with friends. In doing so we sustain and enrich ourselves and everyone around us.

# CHAPTER ELEVEN

# *Loving Oneself*

FIRST-CENTURY Rabbi Hillel Hababli wrote: 'If I do not love myself, who am I?' Loving oneself is closely linked to our identity, to our feeling of being a person. The human person is wired for loving, but this loving begins in loving oneself; without it no love ever really grows. And our ability to love others flourishes as we grow in genuine self-love. Loving oneself is as important for full human living as breath is for life. Defective breathing leads to a poor quality of life, while full deep breathing greatly enhances it. Likewise, the ability to love oneself deeply and authentically leads to a rich feeling of self-worth, and a strong ability to love others.

In the fourth century BC, the Greek philosopher, physician and scientist, Aristotle, wrote: 'Our love for ourselves is the model and root of friendship, because our friendship for others consists precisely in the fact that our attitude towards them is the same as our attitude towards ourselves. Like him, in the thirteenth century, Thomas Aquinas wrote: 'Friendly feelings towards others flow from a person's own friendly feelings towards himself'. We cannot accept love from others if we feel that we ourselves are unlovable. Self-love is essential to selfhood. Without it, the self has a permanent feeling of being deprived, hungry, starved.

Before divorces take place, spouses often hear statements like, 'You are not the person I married'. These disappointed spouses claim that they no longer recognize the person towards whom they were attracted and whom they thought they loved.

If married love is to endure, it is clearly important to know well the person one is loving. This takes time. For the same reason, it is important that we know ourselves well, lest we waste our lives loving an image, a shadow or a dream, instead of our real selves.

True love of oneself begins with accurate self-knowledge, and especially with an ability to be conscious of our own feelings. Unless we know our values, our assumptions, our biases and our fears, we will filter our experience of others through these, and then imagine that our experiences are present in others. By the time we reach adulthood, our feelings have developed a pattern which is fairly predictable and unlikely to change very much as we grow older. Throughout our lives, most of us continue to have similar feeling-reactions to similar situations. To some degree, the same things continue to make us feel happy or sad, peaceful or angry, content or anxious. Being able to recognise our present thought-paradigms or our own very personal repertoire of feelings is essential for authentic self-love.

Unless we have well-founded self-knowledge, we will live with a continually confused identity on which it is impossible to build real love. Unless we can also recognize and name our attitudes, our feelings and our underlying assumptions, we do not know ourselves and who is the 'I' that we are trying to love.

This is especially true of our prejudices through which we filter so many of our judgements. What we push under the carpet of our consciousness eventually trips us up in our steps towards accurate self-knowledge. Deep reflection alone, or with the help of a close friend who will speak truthfully to us, are sources of this self-knowledge, without which fully authentic love of ourselves is impossible.

After self-knowledge comes the gradual process of self-acceptance, and it can be stressful to reach this stage. Even to accept our positive feelings and better virtues can be difficult for us. In his inaugural speech, President Nelson Mandela said:

> Our deepest fear is not that we are inadequate. Our deepest fear is that we are powerful beyond measure. It is our light, not our darkness, that frightens us most. We ask ourselves, who am I to be more successful and more attractive to others? Actually who are you not to be? Your playing small does not save the world. There is nothing enlightened about being shrinking, so that other people will not feel insecure around you. We were born to make manifest the glory of God that is within us. When we are liberated from our fears, our presence automatically liberates others. Our fears often blur or even bury our lovable strengths.

It can often be more difficult to accept our weaknesses; but to accept that we are imperfect is part of human happiness, just as to accept the imperfection of others is part of human happiness also. If we fail to accept our weaknesses, we will spend our lives trying to love a faultless person who does not exist. Real love of ourselves proceeds from self-knowledge and a self-acceptance that tolerantly recognises and loves ourselves at our present level of development. St Paul says that each one of us is 'God's work of art' (Ephesians 2:10). And as we grow older, it is worth remembering that works of art always become more beautiful and valuable with age.

This quiet acceptance of ourselves, at the level of development we have reached. does not mean a self-satisfied unwillingness to grow, to continue developing our desirable qualities and to lessen our undesirable ones. While accepting ourselves at our present stage of perfection or of imperfection, we each need a healthy desire and determination to move on, to grow patiently towards being our better selves. This does not mean becoming a replica of someone else, be they parent, friend or favourite saint. No one has ever been like you, and no model for your complete imitation exists. Situations limit us but they cannot paralyse us into stagnation. Nothing great was ever achieved except by those who dared to believe that some power inside them was superior to circumstances. This self-loving determination to grow remains in us until we consciously or subconsciously choose to accept an undeveloped selfhood.

The effort to grow in loving ourselves is taken in small steps and, we need to encourage ourselves as we calmly take these steps. Time can diminish our ideals unless we constantly challenge ourselves to renew them. Our search for growth must always exceed our present grasp, but as we age, an ever widening gap can develop between what we once aspired to grasp and the reality of what we are able to reach. We are always tempted to relinquish our desire to grow. When we notice this gap between what we are and what we could become, we grow in realism, in humility and in self-respect. This is love of oneself. Michelangelo put it this way: 'Lord, that I may always desire more than I can accomplish'.

Hope is not the conviction that something will turn out well. Rather it is the certainty that something is worth doing. Unless we are failing from time to time in doing the worthwhile, we are probably working below capacity. Parting from our comfort zone always hurts a little, but not to part from it is to stagnate in an unexamined life that never risks to distance itself from a lifeless, cosy comfortableness. Even when cold water is thrown on our plans to grow, we can warm it up with self-encouragement, and turn it into a steam power for action. Loving ourselves involves accepting ourselves as unique individuals with unrivalled promise. There is unfinished growth in all of us.

Desiring to love ourselves by thinking vaguely about how to be happier, or just how to be more comfortable by making woolly resolutions, is not true self-love. Real love of ourselves expresses itself in doing something that enables growth. You are already doing it by reading this book or any other book about meaning and self-improvement. There are many useful courses that help physically, emotionally and mentally. The greatest obstacle to growth is not ignorance; it is the illusion that we know everything, or it is the decision to cease wanting to learn more. Listening to someone you trust, who desires your total wellbeing, and who encourages or challenges you, is a powerful growth-giving exercise.

Many of us need to be reminded, hopefully by a friend, that we fail to love ourselves by feeling that we are a *has-been*, when, deep down, we are a *won't be*. The practice of loving self-growth is not an elevator; it is a ladder. Much stagnation and illness is due to neglect of the simple axiom, 'Use it or lose it'. The 'it' here refers to the muscles of our bodies, the cells of our brain or our appreciation of beauty. If we ever think we are too old to start growing, it is worthwhile to ask ourselves: if I start now, what age will I be if I make the effort and achieve my expected level. Then ask ourselves what age will I be if I make no effort and fail to reach my goal.

We have all learned that, despite our desires and good intentions to grow, we will often fail. Our hopes for ourselves seem so intense, our plans so firm, and yet our perseverance is often so flabby. Real love of ourselves expresses itself in a desire and determination to begin again after our failures if the task is worth doing. It does not mean never having failed. The only real failure takes place when, having failed, we lose the desire to start again when the goal is really achievable.

The core of who we are expresses itself in the small, often unnoticed, moral beginning-again moments in daily life. This calls for patient love of ourselves, and for frequent self-forgiveness. To feel regretful when we fail through human weakness, or to feel guilty when we fail deliberately, is healthy. However, feelings of prolonged regret or of protracted guilt are both unhealthy. Notice that we are more often willing to forgive others than to forgive ourselves. To love ourselves is to pardon ourselves constantly, to have an attitude of mercy towards ourselves, lest we begin to live weighed down with the burden of guilt.

True self-love thrives when we fully accept our talents or gifts, and we celebrate them. This celebration begins when we feel grateful for all the goodness and giftedness within us. Life itself is unearned, and if we have a reason to live, a reason to die, good health-at-age, real friends, a home to live in, food to nourish us, work we like doing and something to hope for, then we are probably in the top 2% of blessed people in the world. Gratitude and celebration can be our only response. And we need to remember that we are not grateful because we are happy; rather we are happy when we are grateful. Gratitude comes before happiness and generates it in abundance.

This rhyme is helpful:

As you wander on through life, whatever be your goal,
keep your eye upon the doughnut and not upon the hole.

There is so much unrecognized doughnut in most of our lives that it is nothing short of unnecessary blindness to concentrate on the holes. When we are weary and we have dishes to wash, we need to remind ourselves that we had food to put on them.

When someone says 'It's an awful day', we need to remind them that it is just raining; it is not an earthquake, a hurricane, a tsunami or a drought. We need to continue to love ourselves into constant growth with a positive outlook, remembering that not all the darkness in the world can extinguish a single candle. And, we always need to remember that life is not a dress rehearsal; no one ever gets a re-play.

# CHAPTER TWELVE

# *The Love of Friendship*

THERE are many levels or depths of friendship. Dr Robin Dunbar, a psychologist at Oxford University, has been study-ing Facebook's connection with the brain for many years. In January 2016, he wrote that claiming to have vast numbers of Facebook friends does not say much about one's actual human relationships. He pointed out that maintaining over a hundred friendships face-to-face consumes a lot of time.

In order to clarify what the word 'friendship' means, he made some useful distinctions, showing that the limits to any individual's number of friends are grounded in the neurology of the cortex. Though Facebook permits 5,000 connections, the average number of human connections is 155, and Dunbar's research showed that 155 is a rough measure of the number of stable relationships that individuals can maintain. This is now called the Dunbar Number.

However, his most recent research shows that the number of those whom you could call real friends, what he called a sym-pathy group, is about 15. He further claims that the number of people you could rely on in a crisis is about five. He refers to that number as a support group. This analysis a useful categorization of kinds of friendship: 155 who might loosely be called friends, 15 who have some sympathetic feeling for us, and five who are ready to help us spontaneously when we are in need.

We know that friendship is a necessary and a positive experi-ence. We need and we enjoy friends. To attain healthy human fulfilment without friendship is impossible. Augustine wrote:

'Whenever people are without a friend not a single thing in the world is friendly to them'. As noted in earlier chapters, doctors, sociologists and psychologists generally agree that alienation is the pathology of our age; in other words, loneliness contributes greatly to any illness in that it can slow down the healing process and in some cases actually cause illness.

We all know what friendship is when we have experienced it. The lack of a good and loyal friend is a sort of psychological nakedness, a constant bleak experience that in turn diminishes a person. The greatest violence we can do to a person is to leave him or her friendless if we could, given our circumstances and our abilities, in some way relate positively to that person.

To have a place in someone's heart is never to be alone. Friends keep us more alive. French novelist, Anaïs Nin, wrote: 'Each friend represents a world within us, a world possibly not born until he or she arrived. At this meeting, a new world is born in us'. There are many worlds waiting to be born in people who lack friends. A new richness is born when friendship happens, a richness which neither person had previously experienced.

The experience of friendship is a sense of caring about another, and being cared for by the other. There is an ease of contact and communication. Friends enjoy each other's company and look forward to any contact or time spent together. To know that I have someone who looks forward to meeting me and who enjoys my company is always an enriching experience. Robert Louis Stephenson said that no one is useless when he or she has a friend. But the experience is infinitely more than that, because a friend tells me that I am not just useful but that I am valuable, important, held in high esteem and cherished.

To love another can sometimes be a demanding and courageous decision. It can even be devoid of any positive feelings, as when we act to help a person who annoys us, who has hurt us, or to whom we are not naturally drawn. Friendship is different in that it includes love, and begins with a positive feeling between two people, a feeling of being at ease with the other. Something flows between friends. It may be a common interest or mutual support or it may be a reciprocated admiration of gifts seen in each other that begins the friendship. Sometimes, friendship develops as the result of an illness or of some other suffering shared. The friendship flourishes as each one recognizes that there is something growthful and enjoyable developing in the relationship for both. Self-disclosure is essential in friendship, even if it does not reach the almost total openness of close intimacy. The love of friendship is facilitated by the qualities enjoyed in the other.

Friendship is permeated by a readiness to accept the other as different and does not attempt to possess or take over the other person. Between friends, the differences in personality, in intelligence, in skills and of opinions might be described as complementary when they stretch and enrich the other person. Friendship love allows for different points of view to be shared and discussed without enmity, because tolerance permeates the relationship. There is an openness, a readiness to trust, and a mutual acceptance of differences among friends that does not exist among acquaintances.

True friends can disturb one another in a very healthy way as they invite one another to grow. Each one's love for the other motivates a desire to move away from harmful attitudes or practices, towards more fruitful living, and towards a greater enjoyment of life. When this challenge to grow takes place, friendships that are less authentic or less mature could come to an end. If the two people are mature, the momentary stress of being challenged can be endured and profited from for growth. This loving willingness to invite a friend to grow must include a willingness to help the growthful process in whatever way we can. A friend is someone who leaves us with every freedom except the freedom not to grow.

The real beauty of friendship is not only in the spontaneous handshake, in the welcoming smile or in the comfort of companionship. It is mainly the experience of warm wholeness we discover when we know that another person cares about our welfare, and is willing to make some sacrifices to enhance it. If we love someone, we can call them to greatness; we can set them free even to leave us. If they are set free and their love is authentic, they will stay with us or come back to us. If they leave us permanently they were never really free or never really our friend.

To help someone lovingly can sometimes cause pain. Friends can hurt each other unintentionally. We are all susceptible to being hurt, and friends recognize this possibility as they gradually share each other's vulnerabilities, admit the areas of sensitivity between them, and forgive each other comfortably. Ordinary friendship can then grow to close intimacy.

As we have seen, friendship-love is a permanent experience of celebration. The peace and joy of knowing that I have a sympathetic or supportive friend whom I can call, email, Skype or visit when I want to, and who can do the same with me, is an enduring source of happiness. Friends like to meet or to make contact as often as they can, and neglecting to do so is often the beginning of the friendship disappearing. Poet and essayist Ralph Emerson advises: 'Go often to a friend's house, because weeds choke up an unused path'.

Friendship memories are strong. Many Jewish people in

the Auschwitz death camp remained determined to stay alive because they were sustained by the memory of a friendship with someone whom they could no longer contact. Sometimes their loved friend was already dead but they did not know it. Friendship-love is enhanced by times of togetherness away from stress, from pressure of work and even from others, but it can also be strengthened during shared stressful moments.

Very simply, friends look forward to any communication, but especially to meeting together in almost any circumstances. They generally feel relaxed when they meet and they feel better after it. Some of these encounters are like hill climbing in beautiful countryside on a bright day; they are exhausting and exhilarating at the same time. Friendship is often built on admiration of each other's minds, but often it is to admire with the heart also.

Yet, friends must allow each other times of privacy, of time spent apart. Friends must respect each other's need to be alone or to be with other friends. It is a deep truth that we cannot possess what we love. This is because all love must be free and liberating, always enabling the other to grow or even grow away from someone who loves them. Any attempt to possess or to limit the other will make for a limping relationship or end up in a broken one.

Promises may attract friends but performance keeps them. A long series of small thoughtless actions can diminish any friendship. Pulitzer Prize winner, Edna St Vincent Millay, wrote: 'It's not that love's going hurt my days but that it went in little ways'. Likewise, a constant desire to force friends into involvement in our interests to the neglect of their own pursuits can contribute to a separation. In one way, friends must be continually re-chosen with humility and with respect for the otherness of the other.

It is as unwise to take a friendship for granted as it is to think that it can be developed without effort. Friendship shines most clearly when it is polished up with some regularity. Modern technology facilitates this consistent contact. Silence in one another's company can be a rich practice among friends, but there are times too when friendship needs a voice. This is especially true when one friend is in trouble. Martin Luther King said: 'In the end, we will remember not the words of our enemies, but the silence of our friends. Did I speak up for my friend when he or she needed me?'

Here are some simple but thought-generating lines about friendship:

When things don't come out right, a friend comes in.

When none of my dreams fail to be true, a friend will surely be.

A friend never gets in your way except to clear it.

A friend never looks for your money unless you've lost it.

Nothing is more important to a friend than making you important.

When you are cornered, he or she is with you in the corner.

A friend always turns up when you are turned down.

All a friend wants in return for a helping hand is your handshake.

A friend remembers gifts received and forgets gifts given.

The love of friendship may not make the world go around but it certainly makes our journey within it more enjoyable. What saves a lot of people from despair is that friends rush in where angels fear to tread.

# CHAPTER THIRTEEN

# The Love of
# Intimate Friendship

FRIENDSHIP-LOVE can be deep and enduring, but there is a deeper and more enduring love. It is called *intimacy-love*. Although it is ideal if married and committed partners possess it, it does not imply sexual intimacy, nor is it limited to male-female relationships. Most people have love in their lives, but not everyone has close intimacy-love. This level of love can be had with one or two other people.

One of the greatest modern psychologists, Erik Erikson, in his book *Identity and the Life Cycle*, describes it as 'the capacity to commit oneself to concrete affiliations, and to the ethical strength to abide by such commitments even when they call for significant sacrifice'. This description stresses that intimacy is not a dreamy, merely emotional or passing experience. It is based on 'concrete affiliations', that is, on real, visible relationships between people. It is not a passive experience, nor is it a passing event. It does not depend on pleasant feelings as friendship-love does, even though these are usually present. Intimate love is founded on a commitment, on a definite decision to trust and to act consistently in a certain way towards another person.

All friendships, but especially intimacy, demand that those involved live out the delicate balance between separateness and connectedness. To meet the challenge of sustaining both of these in the closeness of intimacy, it is necessary that each person has a strong sense of their own identity. That is why, unlike instant coffee, there is no such thing as instant intimacy; it grows slowly. If partners in intimacy can never confront each other, it is not intimacy. Intimate friends can speak deeply and openly in total trust about things that are important to each of them. This level of trust involves an ease and a readiness to take an open stand on any subject. Clear identities allow each person to state unambiguously the limits of their tolerance for mutual behaviour and for verbal exchange, especially if these are emotional issues. People with a strong sense of identity allow others to think, feel or believe differently, without feeling threatened or forced to change. Neither person forces the other to remain silent about any issue. Each can share his or her weaknesses with the other, without fear of ridicule or of experiencing a feeling of inferiority.

Erikson states that not everyone is capable of this level of trust, only those who have what he describes as 'the ethical strength'. This ethical strength can be described as moral courage or strong determination and generosity of heart to stay with the demands of a very close relationship. This strength continues to support the other when positive feelings might not be present, as they are for most of the time in friendship-love. People who shed friendships easily when they are demanding, or people who use others for their own benefit, can never reach intimacy.

The deeper reason for this is that intimacy-love is always ready to accept the need for 'significant sacrifice' when the other's welfare would benefit from it. Unlike friendship-love, intimacy-love does not come to an end easily. Each of the two people involved is prepared to suffer seriously for the good of the other and for the relationship if it becomes necessary. For all these reasons, the happiness of intimacy-love is a great achievement and a precious gift when it is achieved. Intimacy-love is for mature people only, and it does not depend on one's sexuality or on either person's social status or intelligence. As in friendship-love, positive feelings can strengthen intimacy-love and usually accompany it, but intimacy-love does not depend on feelings.

Intimate friends say something like this to each other: 'I will strive to understand all that you are. I will share with you in all that I am. I will trust you no matter what. I will support you in all that you do. I will help you in all your needs. I will encourage you in all your endeavours. I will love you in all that you are, while encouraging and actively helping you to become your best self.' Even if these words are not actually spoken, intimate friends know that, if they were spoken, they would express what is honestly present between them. It must be obvious that this is a description of many marriages and of many relationships between single people or between opposite and same-sex friends. The commitment to intimacy-love has great rewards. Here is how Dinah Maria Craik describes it:

> Oh, the inexpressible comfort of feeling safe with a person, neither having to weigh thoughts nor measure words, but to pour them all out just as they are, chaff and grain together, knowing that a faithful hand will take and sift them, keeping what is worth keeping, and with a breath of kindness blow the rest away.

The beauty of intimate love is the together-strength which comes when I discover that another person believes in me and trusts me totally. To have this intimate place in someone's heart is never to be alone nor ever to foresee loneliness while both of us are alive.

An intimate friend is someone who knows you as you are,

understands where you have come from, accepts who you have become, and invites you to grow. Karl Rahner, a Jesuit priest, gives his own experience:

> When I suddenly have the experience of personal love and encounter, I become startled and blessed in both at once. The fact is that I have been accepted with a love that is absolute and unconditional and I am unable to find any justification for it in my own finitude and frailty. Thus too it is when I experience that I likewise love with an inconceivable audacity which overcomes all questions about the other.

This deep mutual love never ceases to grow, because it continually discovers more beauty in the depths of the other. In human loving we see fully only what we love, and the more we see, the more we love.

We must have 'found ourselves' before we can share ourselves in the demanding situation of intimacy. Unlike friendship-love, close intimate love accepts all that a person is. From a theologian who based his theology on anthropology, Karl Rahner, we receive this wisdom: 'Authentic loving is giving the whole of oneself. In this act alone, each of us possesses ourselves completely.'

The German pastor and martyr, Dietrich Bonhoeffer, wrote: 'The person who cannot be alone should beware of being in community with others, and the person who is not in communion with others should beware of being alone.' If I cannot be alone, I cannot be intimate. Children, adolescents and immature people are not capable of intimacy; they are dependent persons. Erikson says that it is only at about the age of 30 that the crisis of Isolation vs Intimacy is resolved and that the capacity for intimacy is reached. Many people never reach it.

Ideally, marriage is founded on intimacy, but neither an ostentatious wedding nor intense sexual behaviour presume or automatically bring adult intimacy. Passion can be fiercely focused and passing, but intimate friendship is calmer, enduring and more open to growing possibilities. It is strictly adults-only territory.

Intimate love is never a bargaining situation; it cannot be a market place. Nor can it be a situation where one person nurses the other; both people must have left the cradle a long time ago. Intimate love is not mere mutual admiration; it is not an art gallery situation. This love cannot be bought or sold, as neither person is a banker. Nor is there any fusion of the two people involved; each must retain and grow in his or her uniqueness. Intimacy is not the same as passionate intensity. It is open to growing possibility, while passion is focused in limited space and time. Intimate love is a moral experience, not just an incandescent happening. Even while loving intimately, friends continue to challenge and to help each other in their development. However, intimacy is not a therapeutic situation nor can intimate friends be drugs for each other against the stress of life. Neither is one friend addicted to the other; they are each freely committed to the other. No win-lose situations arises because no games are played.

Sexual attraction can be the beginning of love, and sexual intimacy can express and deepen love but, of themselves, neither is intimacy nor love. Love may or may not include sexual attraction. Sexual activity could accompany hatred or contempt or indifference or selfish use of the other. Erickson reminds us that, unless there is a capacity for intimacy in a relationship, it could remain 'dominated by phallic or vaginal strivings that make sex-life a kind of genital combat'.

It has been said that a person who does not understand the silence of the other will never understand their words. Intimate lovers hear the silence of the other's unique beauty, below any evidence of their weaknesses. This is why the deeper intimate love becomes, the more easily friends can sit silently together. They experience each other not as objects or finished products, but as human beings on a journey, and in the process of growing together. In this way, they live with a continual sense of surprise and wonder, knowing that each meeting is a new discovery of the other.

As the world-expert on the subconscious, psychiatrist Carl Jung, put it, 'Where love reigns there is no will to power'. People who love intimately resist all forms of domination. Intimate love is always by invitation, never by obligation or regulation. Some religions forget this, reducing faith and love to obligations and commandments. Of course it takes much greater strength to love someone than to dominate them. Mature intimate friends can hold on tightly and, no matter how painful, they can let go lightly when the other's good requires it. Intimate friends wish each other to be happy even more than they desire to be together.

Intimate love has its priorities clear and the first of those is the welfare of the other. This selflessness is tested when one person needs some time alone or apart, as all healthy people do. Poet Patrick Kavanagh advises about the need for this sacred distance even between close friends: 'We've tasted too much, lover. Through a chink too wide there comes no wonder'. All genuine friends give each other space. Lebanese American artist and poet Kahil Gibram also counsels us: 'Let there be space in your togetherness'. Bertrand Russell reminds us, 'Absence diminishes weak love and it increases great love, as the wind extinguishes tapers but adds fury to fire'. Each meeting is a discovery because both people are always growing. There is a quiet excitement because they are different each time they meet. The same words may be used or similar gestures shown but intimate love always sees the more. At the same time, intimacy depends on deep mutual respect so that, while each person encourages the other to grow, neither pushes the other beyond their area of comfort. Even in the most intimate friendship, there is a deep part of each individual that cannot be touched by anyone. Intimate love always respects, hopes and waits lovingly. It lives and thrives on openness, sharing, availability, dependability, trust, lack of fear, and on mutually revealed vulnerability.

# CHAPTER FOURTEEN

# Love Is Self-transcendence

EVERY time we show love to someone, we share something of ourselves – our thoughts, our emotions, our time, our energy or our possessions. When we do – unless we do it for totally selfish reasons – we reach beyond ourselves; we transcend ourselves. It is always a choice, because we do not have to do it. In the free world, we are always at liberty to make the decision not to reach out to others with our time, our talents or our gifts. Animals stay with and defend their young, and swans are faithful to their partner until death. But they are not free *not* to do it; they are compelled and controlled by instinct. Unlike them, we *are* free to show concern for others' welfare. When we act for the other's welfare, it is a chosen or freely decided commitment to do so. It is reaching out in self-transcendence.

This willingness to transcend ourselves and our self-interest is quite common. Good parents and grandparents do it every day. Many people give anonymously to charity; thousands give free time to engage our youth in sporting organizations. Others engage in a selfless struggle to gain justice for the poor. People have died while trying to pull others from burning buildings, and soldiers have thrown their bodies on live grenades to save comrades. Every day, each of us shows love in numerous small acts of kindness, generosity and patience with our families and our circle of friends. These acts are often conscious or subconscious, spontaneous or slow decisions. They are commitments to behave in ways that are contrary to our immediate or long-term self-interest.

Psychological research offers growing evidence that these, sometimes painful, selfless decisions, are very often accompanied by the presence of positive emotions. It is not difficult to recall times in our lives when, having acted generously, but against immediate fears or inclinations, we felt well. Most of the time there is a built-in response, a good feeling that rewards us when we know that we did the noble but difficult thing. Besides this principled action, people who love in this way are much more admired and popular than those who live by the self-interest model.

But deeper still, these self-transcending decisions enhance our own feeling of self-worth. When we reach emotional adulthood, there is a force built into our nature that favours our acting contrary to immediate self-gratification. There is an other-directed desire deep in us to suppress our selfishness and to act selflessly towards others even when we do not feel like doing so. To be aware of our own flaws makes selfless loving behaviour much easier.

This awareness of how generous behaviour builds up our sense of selfhood does not force us to be patient, kind or generous. However, when we reach adulthood – which does not always come automatically with age – we become aware of this other-directed thrust within us, and we grow in our ability to reach beyond mere self-interest. Children or immature people cannot be expected to recognize this other-directed thrust because the ability to transcend themselves has not yet been fully developed in them. Mature people, however, know that the self-interest model of human activity provides a woefully inadequate pattern for fullness of living. The positive view of human nature provides a much more effective and enduring model than sharing only when it fits into our time schedule or when threats of punishment in civil courts or rewards in an afterlife are present.

When we compare the 'me-first' or 'me-only' selfish person with the generous person the difference is obvious; and when we ourselves are generous, especially if we do not have to be, it is clearer still. The 'what's-in-it-for-me' person is never really happy, whereas generous people are. Darwin's theory on the survival of the fittest has driven material evolution, but it does not control or assure the integral growth of the human species. On the contrary, as Aldous Huxley wrote: 'The individual can achieve self-fulfilment only by self-transcendence'. Teilhard de Chardin articulated the same sentiment when he wrote: 'Love is a secret reserve of energy. It is the blood of spiritual evolution'. Nobel prize-winning Indian philosopher Rabindranath Tagore put it this way: 'I dreamt that life was joy, I awoke and saw that it was service. I acted and discovered that service was joy'. Takers ultimately lose; givers win in the long run. Holocaust survivor Martin Grey expressed this well in his book, *For Those I Have Loved*, when he wrote: 'He or she who gives much receives much, because, at a deep level, we possess what we give away'

South African Anglican bishop Desmond Tutu reminded us of an African concept, *Ubuntu / botha,* which tries to describe the essence of being human by saying that a person is a person only with and through other persons. He says that men or women who think they are totally self-sufficient are sub-human, and that we all need to connect caringly with other human beings to be fully human. A human person is not just a rational animal; each person is a relating, loving, meaning-seeking being, and that meaning is found in reaching beyond, in transcending ourselves to connect lovingly with others. To confirm our existence as persons, as distinct from our physical existence, seventeenth-century philosopher René Descartes wrote the famous sentence; '*Cogito, ergo sum.*' (I think, therefore I exist). However, humanistic psychologists like Maslow would say: 'I love, therefore I exist and grow as a person' Stressing that humans are essentially socially oriented, they are saying that it is only in so far as I love that I am a person.

In her book on human growth, *Passages,* researcher and writer Gail Sheehy says: 'An exclusive concern with self runs directly counter to the evidence that emerged from my research. My consistent finding is that the highest-satisfaction people were devoted to some cause or purpose beyond themselves.' Poet and novelist D.H. Lawrence wrote: 'As we live we are transmitters of life, and when we fail to transmit life, life fails to flow through us. However, giving life is not easy. It means kindling the life-quality where it was not'. Psychiatrist Scott Peck summarizes these thoughts briefly: 'True fulfilment is, I believe, vicarious.'

During a lecture, I asked Viktor Frankl what he, as a Jewish psychiatrist, considered the source of and the motivation for moral behaviour. He replied with three questions given him by a rabbi, which he said could be answered only by people who have reached moral adulthood, that is, the ability to transcend themselves. These are:

- If I don't love you, *who* will give you the love I denied you?
- If I don't love you now, *when* will I give you the love I denied you now?
- If I do not love you or act lovingly towards you for totally selfish reasons, *what* am I?

When he had given us time to reflect on our personal responses to these questions, he said that the answer to the first question was 'No one', because no other person can ever give you the unique love I could have given you. To the second question, his answer was, 'Never', because while I can love you later, it can never be the love I could have given you earlier.

Frankl's answer to the third question was that the individual had behaved as animals do, because animals cannot freely choose to transcend themselves in concern for the other. It is clear that real love cannot be motivated by law or by an institution. There is a deep desire within the mature person to transcend oneself in loving actions, and an equally deep satisfaction at having brought happiness to another.

Forced, commanded or legislated moral behaviour can hardly be called appealing; in fact, it could doubtfully be called moral. To see, to recognize, and to follow our interior thrust towards a self-transcending lifestyle is clearly beautiful. As St Augustine wrote: 'In as much as love grows within you, so does beauty, because love is the beauty of the soul.' St. John emphasized the negative and unhealthy effect of failure to love: 'If a person does not love, he or she holds fast by death' (1 *John* 3:14.) Although this is primarily a faith-statement, it is also a valid and important psychological insight. Loving self-transcendence is life-giving to the one who gives love and to the receiver. Its absence leads to unhappiness in both people. It is not where I breathe that I live; it is where I love. Growth, human development takes place when we fully accept the giftedness of ourselves, and begin to share that gift with others. If in doubt, it is always wiser and more beautiful to do the loving thing.

In rather technical language, the American theologian John Courtney Murray wrote: 'Love is centripetal, that is, it returns to enrich the giver. It is also centrifugal as it moves out towards the other in a creative way.' Love given passes on from the giver to the receiver, enabling that person in turn to pass it on to others. Love given has no happy ending because love given never ceases to transmit itself.

It is interesting that one of the words we use most frequently, even when passing by others, expresses a wish to transcend ourselves in concern for them. It is the word *Hello.* In Old English it was spelt *hal beo thu,* meaning 'may you be whole, or blessed'. However casually we use it, when meant sincerely it is a wish that the people we greet will be fully developed, whole. It expresses our desire that they will transcend themselves even for a moment, by wishing them fullness of life. It is not a difficult habit to become conscious of the word's significance each time we say *Hello.*

In his book, *Man's Search for Meaning,* Victor Frankl wrote: 'By virtue of the self-transcendence of human existence, man is a being in search of meaning. Self-transcendence is one of the basic features of human existence. Only when man withdraws from himself, in the sense of letting self-centred interest and attention go, will he gain an authentic mode of existence'. And in his book *The Unconscious God* he wrote: 'Transcendence refers to the very highest and most inclusive or holistic levels of human consciousness. It means behaving and relating to other people, to oneself, to significant others, to human beings in general, to other species, to nature and to the cosmos, as ends in themselves, rather than as means'. This is self-transcendent loving.

Most of the time, all of us can join with the poet Patrick Kavanagh when he expresses the thought: 'It's time to throw away my sticky self. Prometheus calls me on, away from me, to go on the grand tour to explore life free of self.'

Comparing falling in love with real love, Scott Peck described self-transcending love in these words:

> Falling in love is not an extension of one's limits or boundaries; it is a partial and temporary collapse of them. The

extension of one's limits requires effort; falling in love is effortless. Lazy and undisciplined individuals are as likely to fall in love as energetic and dedicated ones. When limits are extended or stretched, they tend to stay stretched. Real love is a permanently self-enlarging experience.

This is a good reason to do the loving thing always, even when no one is looking.

For Christian believers, the deepest and final experience of self-transcendence is to give oneself to God in love. On this subject, St John assures us that 'God is love and those who abide in love, abide in God and God abides in them' (1 *John* 4:16).

# CHAPTER FIFTEEN

# *Love and Enjoyment*

ONE OF the greatest confusions about love is to equate it with an enjoyable feeling. 'I love that wine', 'Don't you love that dress?', 'I really love travel', 'Everyone loves the way John speaks', 'I love that piece of music', 'I love driving my car', 'You will really love that cheese'. None of these statements express real love as a willingness to transcend ourselves for another's wellbeing. Ideally, the word here would be 'enjoy'; 'I *enjoy* beer, travel, my car, cheese, music, pleasant people or an interesting book.

Love is reaching out towards another person; enjoyment is a pleasant feeling within oneself. It is a pleasant everyday experience to enjoy good company or such things as books, scenery, works of art, tasty food or activities like walking, playing tennis, or watching football. Love and enjoyment of other persons often go together but they are not the same; they are separable experiences. We can enjoy people we do not love and we can love people we do not enjoy. Of course it is always easier to love those whose company we enjoy, and more difficult to love someone whose company we do not enjoy. Basically, loving is giving, while enjoying is receiving. Loving is reaching out to others, while enjoying is accepting a pleasant experience from others, or from a situation.

The confusion between the words is understandable because loving is often very enjoyable. However, when a parent lovingly stays up for most of the night with a sick child it is not an enjoyable experience. Nor is it enjoyable when a wife gives up a planned evening out in order to stay at home with her depressed husband or when a husband loves his wife enough to respond patiently when she has hurt him. To love is often enjoyable, but sometimes it is not. Even when loving and enjoying exist together, they can be looked at as different and separable experiences also.

If I enjoy you, *you* are an enjoyable person, but if I love you, *I* am a loving person. Enjoyment could be described as a gift *from* the other, while loving is a gift *to* the other. I can enjoy people whom I do not love, as when I enjoy a TV entertainer whom I may not love because he or she has been proven dishonest. And I can love people whom I don't enjoy. To love is a decision; to enjoy is a feeling.

Loving is seldom an isolated action. It comes from an attitude within the loving person. The loving attitude flows into loving actions. In other words, if I am a loving person, I am living with a fairly consistent, loving attitude towards people. This loving or unloving attitude usually stems from our parents' attitude towards us in our earliest years. If parents have failed to love their children, the children can have great difficulty in showing love or accepting love from others. These disadvantaged children will need to be loved more than usual, but often without being able to offer much enjoyment to those who love them. Yet, unloved people are lovable if we have the patience and tolerance to look deeply, and to remember that their unpleasant qualities have been built into them by prolonged deprivation or maltreatment early in their lives. It is surprising how a consistent loving acceptance and forgiveness can change the image of unloveableness in people who have been hurt deeply.

Of course, all love that grows usually begins with some mutual enjoyment. While love is not merely feeling attracted to a person, it often begins to develop when one feels drawn towards another because of his or her neediness. Love may begin by the enjoyment of looking at the other person's beautiful face, listening to the other person's clear thinking, admiring their skills, feeling their insecurity or, most likely of all, the other person's interest in me. Love can follow a first meeting, as the inward feeling of enjoyment becomes an outward expression of our readiness to love. Yet our love for another can emerge, despite another's unpleasant and unenjoyable qualities, if I am a loving person.

In this connection the Italian language has two phrases: *Ti voglio bene*, meaning 'I wish you well', and the more popular *Ti amo*, meaning 'I love you'. Referring to a bottle of wine, an Italian would never say either *Ti amo* or *Ti voglio bene*. They would say *Mi piace*, 'I like it' or 'I enjoy it' about their favourite wine. They express love for another best in a phrase, *Ti voglio bene*.

To compare the meanings of enjoying and of loving further, we can say that enjoyment results from an attraction, while love can result from a desire and leads to a decision to help another person in some way. This desire to help another goes beyond any positive or negative feeling about the person loved. In other words, we can act lovingly towards a very unattractive person. I cannot be attracted to everyone, nor can I enjoy everyone, but if I am a mature loving person, I can act lovingly towards everyone because, within the limits of my time, my energy and my other responsibilities, I can act generously towards unpleasant people for their welfare. My response comes from the fact that I am a caring person, regardless of how enjoyable the other people I meet happen to be.

Enjoyment with another emerges from the enjoyable qualities they manifest and from our own capacity for enjoyment. Loving another comes from our ability to reach beyond ourselves, regardless of the qualities of the people we meet. This is high-quality adult living. It is maturity at its best. Each time we meet another person we can either consciously or subconsciously make a decision to act lovingly. We are then responding maturely. Our loving action is not connected with how enjoyable we find the other person.

There is much that is enjoyable in our daily life experiences. However, enjoyment is not predictable; it comes and goes, and we do not have much control over it. Some of the people we meet are more enjoyable than others. The actions of some people can be very difficult to tolerate. It can be stressful to be in their company because they tend to be anti-social, over-sensitive, aggressive, very selective in their generosity, or because their personality is prickly. Unlike our enjoyment of others, love can be as predictable as we wish it to be because it is a choice that we are always free to make. We can limit our loving but not easily our enjoyment. Love is as reliable as we want it to be, but enjoyment is not as reliable. Shakespeare emphasised the permanence of authentic love when he wrote: 'Love is not love which alters when it alteration finds' (*Sonnet* 116).

When we enjoy something or someone's company, we feel well about them at the time. Sometimes it can be high-quality enjoyment and last a long time, or it can be of a poor quality and can pass quickly. Love can be very deep or less so, but if it was authentic love in the beginning it cannot easily fade away, unless we decide to stop acting lovingly. When we enjoy loving another, the enjoyment can exist most of the time side by side with the loving, but it can also disappear while the loving endures. Both love and enjoyment can help a relationship, but love is much more dependable and successful in sustaining the relationship. The fact that you enjoy another's company does not mean that you love that person. Nor does the fact that you do not enjoy that person's company mean that you are failing to love them.

Enjoyment is a feeling, a very welcome one, but feelings have a certain independence. As discussed in earlier chapters, we cannot control them directly. We cannot command feelings to come or to go; we can deal with them only indirectly, sometimes with success and sometimes not. Most of our feelings are products of the past, but that does not leave us prisoners of the past; feelings can be controlled and even changed over time.

In the deepest meaning of the word 'love', we cannot *fall* in love, because falling is something we never choose to do, while to love or to refuse to love is always within our control. We can certainly have an enjoyable experience when we meet an enjoyable person, but enjoyment cannot always be planned. We can say that enjoyment somehow falls upon us or we fall into enjoyment. It is also easy to fall out of an enjoyable experience. But if loving is a cultivated attitude making us a loving person, it will not easily be reversed. Eighteenth-century Irish novelist Laurence Sterne wrote: 'To say a man or woman has fallen in love or that he or she is deeply in love without having chosen it, carries an implication that authentic love is below a person'.

A friendship founded on the hope of constant mutual enjoyment is a risky adventure, and a marriage thus founded is destined to fail. Only love can sustain any deep human relationship, especially the testing one of life together 'until death do us part'. Yet we know that all healthy friendships and most happy marriages thrive despite moments of lessened enjoyment.

Love and 'falling in love' has been the enduring theme of many enjoyable films. Film critic Frank Pittman recalls the love story in *Casablanca*, featuring Humphrey Bogart and Ingrid Bergman. He says that Bogart had some deathless lines about the enjoyment of sex and romance with Ingrid, but he sends Ingrid back to her husband, Paul Henreid. Bogart gives the impression that he believes freeing France from the Nazis takes priority over the itch he feels for Bergman. He says, 'Ilse, I'm no good at being noble, but it don't not take much to see that the enjoyment of two little people does not amount to a hill of beans in this crazy world.' Bogart is saying that there is something in life that takes priority over personal enjoyment, even the enjoyment of 'falling in love'. Maybe the cost of loving in a lifelong marriage, or making the sacrifice necessary to do something else noble, is that something.

Viktor Frankl lost his parents, his pregnant wife and his brother in the death camp. However, having observed other prisoners, he wrote: 'I lost everything except the last of the human freedoms, which is to choose one's attitude in any given set of circumstances.' He said that he was able to do this, because he still had 'something to do, someone to love and something to hope for.' In the midst of his terrible suffering, he made a decision to dwell on these three goals. If you pursue happiness through enjoyment, it will elude you; but, if you make a loving decision to meet people and their needs, you will find it. Feelings are secondary to this journey.

The core of love is a free decision and a continued discipline to give and to share; it is not an intensity of feeling. It is a moral arena, not just an incandescent experience.

# CHAPTER SIXTEEN

# Identity, Addiction and Love

FINDING our identity, the discovery of who we are, our self-hood and how we are unique, marks the years between 12 and 20. Some lifelong confusion in our vocational choice can result from failure to establish our identity during these years.

Because authentic love is a sharing of ourselves, we cannot love unless we first possess a self to share. Erich Fromm says: 'paradoxically the ability to be alone is the condition for the ability to love'. I cannot give any part of myself in loving another, unless I have first found and know myself. A secure sense of clear, separate identity gives us the power and confidence to share that identity with the other. Each of us must find the strength of our own identity and of our own creative solitude before we begin to share it with another. A feeling of personal confusion about our identity is not a healthy basis for striving to love. We must first find ourselves before we attempt to relate to others in an adult way.

To love, we have to possess a separate, clearly delineated identity that is able and ready to share itself with others in a non-dependent way. When this clearly defined personal identity is achieved, we can then combine a comfortable closeness and relaxed separateness in relating to others. Without it, there would be fusion with the other, or a growing pretence, or even exploitation of the other person. If both people in a relation-ship do not have a reasonably secure identity, there can be an attempt to control the other, or a situation of co-dependency can develop. Real love demands a personal availability to another person, the depth of which depends on the degree of our own self-possession; and this can never be lost as love grows. Love reflects and depends on the degree to which we possess a unique identity and are free to share it with another person. This happens in ways that give the other person access to our inner self, without any personal loss. In fact, this mutual love enriches the identity of both people involved in the relationship.

The discovery of our identity is not sudden or automatic; if it evolves it has been a gradual development. While in the womb, a baby's identity depends totally on its mother. There is no disconnection between mother and baby; the baby experiences fusion and possession. Although the baby is a distinct person, it has no experience of separateness, of a distinct identity. For this reason, the experience of the baby is one of total security and of effortless safety, unless its mother is experiencing prolonged stress. The baby lives in a paradise of pleasure, of fulfilment and of need-satisfaction. The baby has no experience of stress, of the frustrating limits of time, temperature or space. For the baby in the womb there is no conscious relationship, no awareness of being loved, no sense of another.

On leaving the womb, the baby meets and collides with the otherness of temperature, of light and darkness, and the touch of other people. It arrives into a world of imperfection, of insecurity, of limited control, and of delayed need-satisfaction that the baby did not experience in the womb. The feeling of frustration takes over from the comfort and cosiness-on-tap in the womb. The baby is beginning to form a sense of personal identity that is distinct and separate. With patient loving in these early years, parents can facilitate this adjustment process as the baby progresses through childhood, adolescence and into adult identity.

Some parents fail to initiate this beautiful process and unfortunately their children never reach maturity. These deprived children can remain without an adult identity. They are usually described as childish. They grow old, but they never grow up. These unfortunate people can never learn to love wholeheartedly unless they receive serious and prolonged therapeutic counselling.

Those who love must be free to give of themselves, and each of us has a different degree of this freedom to share ourselves with others. Ideally, the loved one is also free to receive. However, some people are not free enough to accept love. They either reject the love given, or they try to possess the one who loves them. Any person who wants to live by loving must be relatively free to make choices. Without this freedom, the dynamic of connectedness and separateness between friends or intimates cannot develop well. The absence or poor quality of personal freedom limits the possibility of healthy friendship, and certainly eliminates the possibility of close intimacy. Life is a journey towards identity and freedom, away from any selfishness that shackles it. All genuine friendship assists people on the journey to an ever-deepening personal freedom.

A healthy friendship can exist only between two people who are without addictive tendencies, in other words, between two people who are free. At the same time, all friendship cultivates deeper freedom in free people. A person who has a strong identity and deep personal freedom will then enable others to have the same experience, while still inviting and encouraging them to grow. Without a good sense of our own identity, there can be a subtle but strong attempt to change the other to our own image and likeness. This attempt would be an invasion of the other's identity and freedom as well as an attempt to fix or to shape the other. On the other hand, a weak sense of identity could result in keeping important issues suppressed rather than having them spoken of and worked on.

Modern society continually releases an avalanche of information on us. This deluge of information has usefully increased the importance of awareness in general, but especially the importance of self-awareness. Misunderstood, however, this increased self-awareness could lead to gradual selfishness in the presence of which a healthy identity cannot develop. The I-ness of identity needs the other-ness of friends. As this exchange grows, both parties feel more appreciated and enhanced. Strengths and weaknesses are not lost sight of in the self or in the other. When identity has developed well, it allows a healthy self-focus. It increases a readiness for open communication and for a profound respecting of differences. It allows a rich emotional connectedness with significant others, in joys and in sorrows, in moments of strength and of weakness. Its foundation will always be the values, beliefs and principles of both parties.

We cannot fully *be*, unless we *be-long*. It is only as we move beyond the self-orientation of childhood and youth and into adult friendships that real self-awareness grows. It is only when we have discovered our identity-awareness that we are able to share freely with other people. When there is an absence of personal identity or a serious vagueness about it, connection with other people tends towards either alienation or addiction. Parents who manifest selfishness or erratic discipline could predispose their children to become addicted in some way. These parents are poor role models.

Addiction in relationships is a need to possess the other in order to sustain our own feeling of emptiness and loneliness. It is a state where we have lost our identity and freedom. In his book, *Care of Mind and Care of Spirit,* psychiatrist Gerald May describes addictions as 'enslavements sucking life energy into specific obsessions and compulsions'. One of the co-founders of Alcoholics Anonymous, Bill Wilson, calls addiction a form of spiritual bankruptcy. In ancient Rome, when a court gave over a person to a master, the words *ad* ('towards') and *dicere* ('to say') were used. This is the origin of the word *addiction.* Someone was given over in slavery to another person's control. This could scarcely be called love, since it is neither a choice, nor is it free.

Compulsive work or the over-use of drugs, alcohol, sex, gambling or of the internet are all well-known forms of addiction. What often happens under the name of friendship or even of intimacy is, in fact, also addiction. It is an outer-directed search for our missing identity, in a partial idolatry of another person. The trouble with all addictions is that they seem to work for a while; there is an immediate pay-off, a pseudo-peace. All addictions serve deep unmet needs in the addict. Addicted people desperately seek pleasure and a sense of escape in substances, in activities or in relationships, because of the great pain of emptiness and lack of harmony within themselves.

This kind of addiction can be a compulsion to use other people as a drug. The person addicted to the company of others feels that there is no one present when others are absent, since they are not present to themselves. Because they have a very frail sense of self, addicted persons seek selfhood in other people and tend to use them for their own satisfaction. Denial and self-centredness are two hallmarks of the addictive process. The deeper reality might be that their addiction stems from a fear of facing a deprived self, without addiction to a substance or to another person. Because there is an inability to establish a relationship with oneself, there is alienation from the self and a drive to seek an obsessive possession of the other person. The addicted person may call this friendship, and sometimes, sadly, it can end in marriage. The addict is always trapped by the feeling of never having enough. Serious therapeutic treatment is vital to deal with this disorder.

Here are useful questions that will help to uncover any addictive tendencies in a friendship:

1. Have you both a feeling of personal security in your own identity, *i.e.* neither of you could be described as a needy person?
2. Do you each encourage the other to have other friends?
3. Do you each allow the other to have personal or private interests?
4. Are you careful not to make the other dependent on you?
5. Do you each desire the other's growth for his or her own sake?
6. Do you both refrain from using the other for selfish reasons?
7. Do you both desire the other's wellbeing, even if this led to ending your relationship?

# CHAPTER SEVENTEEN

# *To Love Is to Sacrifice*

THERE are many words used to describe uncomfortable feelings – pain, irritation, agony, anguish, heartache, misery, torment, torture, tension, suffering and sadness. These words are generally seen as negatives and as feelings to be avoided if possible. The word *sacrifice* is also used loosely to describe unpleasant experiences, but it is different from uncomfortable feelings.

The word *sacrifice* usually describes a discomfort that has been chosen or accepted for noble reasons. Sacrifices are something we choose to 'make'. The Oxford dictionary describes sacrifice as 'the act of giving up something one values, for something that is more important'. The pain or discomfort of giving up something, which sacrifice entails, are not the core of an act of sacrifice. An act of sacrifice has a more positive meaning, as for instance when a young graduate freely gives a few years of unpaid service to help a developing country or when public servants work beyond their duty to help the community. Sacrifice is clearly linked to the giving of oneself and to loving.

In Taipei, I met a young Chinese girl, named Jing Ying, who came from a very poor family. She told me how for many years she appreciated her parents' struggles to find money to have her nicely dressed. Jing Ying told me how her mother spent time washing, mending and ironing her few well-worn dresses, and saving to buy new ones as she grew older. She told me that when her mother replaced her old or torn dress with a clean or mended one, she would always ask her daughter to stand in front of her for a few minutes. On one of these occasions Jing Ying impatiently asked her mother why she had to stand in her clean dress for what seemed, in her childish experience, to be a long time. Her mother answered, 'My darling Jing Ying, it is because I love you and I enjoy looking at my precious daughter'. Jing Ying told me that, at that moment and for the first time, she understood why her mother made many sacrifices for her.

It is understandable that the word 'sacrifice' has a negative ring when we hear the word linked with suicide bombers who kill innocent people, claiming that their sacrifices will secure a place for them in heaven. This word can also conveys a negative feeling when, mistakenly, we understand from biblical stories that God condoned the slaughter of helpless animals or, that he demanded the terrible death of his Son to assuage divine anger. The word *sacrifice* is in great need of being rescued and rehabilitated from false understandings. So often, it sounds harsh and joyless, and it has given religion the same image in the eyes of many. Perhaps it is only by reflection on the human experience of sacrifice that its deepest meaning or even its religious sense can be rescued and understood properly.

We can all see that society could become a bleak experience if voluntary acts of self-giving sacrifice ceased. So many wonderful people give time, work and money, voluntarily and sacrificially, without always enjoying what they do. People give of themselves sacrificially, without any financial reward or recognition, to alleviate suffering in others. Many professional people, who are rewarded for their skilled work, still generously give much more time and effort helping others. We think especially of nurses, doctors, social workers, teachers and clergy, but there are many people like them in every walk of life.

Every human being has three deep needs: security, significance, and solidarity. We are social beings, wired to need physical and emotional security with the help of others. We also need others to help us achieve something significant in our lives. Since 'no man is an island', we each need to know and to feel that we belong, to feel solidarity with family and friends. The satisfaction of these three needs deep within us calls for sacrifices from others. Without selfless help from others, human growth is not fully achieved and a deep level of personal happiness will escape us. Sacrifice is part of healthy, human community everywhere.

Without the feeling that we have people who lovingly make sacrifices for us, even our religious services would be meaningless, because there would no loving community underneath the ritual that speaks about it. Sacrificial loving is not a virtue for saints and heroes; it is a basic human need for individuals and for society. It is interesting to note that, in Hebrew, the word meaning 'to get close to someone or to become friends' and the word meaning 'to sacrifice oneself' have the same root. We find real love only in relationships where there is a readiness for real sacrifice.

The reality is that we humans are dependent creatures whose lives are most enhanced when we share with one another. Sometimes this sharing can be purchased, but it is most effective when done lovingly in freedom. In her book, *Sharing the Darkness*, medical doctor Sheila Cassidy, who was tortured in Chile for helping the wounded and who gave much of her life to hospice work, wrote: 'Loving is a costly business, demanding a radical renunciation of human distaste and prejudice, a gift of self which is often more than we had bargained for'. St Augustine put this comment another way in the phrase, *pondus meus amor meus,* meaning 'my burden is my love' and *pondus amoris,* literally 'the weight, or the burden which accompanies loving'.

He is describing love as a burden, which he accepted gladly.

Loving always implies seeking the welfare or flourishing of the other. This steadfastness often demands curbing our own legitimate desires. Giving our time in listening to others who need it in order to lessen their loneliness or their fears can be a real sacrifice. Very often it is by listening caringly that we enhance the welfare of others, even when we cannot actually do anything external to help.

Sheila Cassidy also wrote:

> What I am arguing for here, when I talk of life, is not for more hospices or more time spent at work, but about a set of attitudes. It is about developing a degree of insight into the patient's world, what psychologists call empathy. With that insight goes a heightened sensitivity into the patient's distress, and searching for ways to relieve it. At heart, professional loving is about competence, empathy and communication. It is about becoming sensitive to the pain of others and therefore making oneself terribly vulnerable. For me, as for many, it is a way of caring which I aspire to, but achieve only some of the time. It is a costly loving for which I am repaid a hundredfold.

When we choose to postpone our personal plans in order to respond to the immediate need of a friend, we are acting sacrificially. So too, when we resist giving the quick sharp response to unkind words, we are loving with sacrifice. Responding with gentleness when harshness could be justified, expresses love in a sacrificial way. Deciding not to respond with verbal or physical aggression, even in self-defence, is another selfless act of love. Simply remaining silent can sometimes be an expression of love, even though that response can be very demanding.

Doing everything possible to deter a son or daughter or a friend from self-harm through overwork, or from taking harmful substances, or from being involved in a risky relationship, is one of the most painful acts of love we can perform. It is even more difficult when our effort fails and the loved one leaves us despite our entreaties. In cases like this we can only wait patiently and pray for their return.

There is a paradox in all loving. When we are not loving we are not fully alive, but when we are loving we are dying to what is not truly human within us. The Dominican Herbert McCabe put this paradox very vividly when he wrote: 'If you do not love, you will not be alive, but if you love, you could die in defence of goodness.' Deaf and blind author Helen Keller put the same profound thought another way: 'Happiness is never attained through self-gratification but through loving and perhaps painful dedication to a worthy cause.' The day we are not 'dying' even a little for others in some way, we are 'dying' even more deeply within ourselves.

There are two possible attitudes to loving; one counts the cost and the other relishes the reward. Sacrifice and the apparent loss are the cost; joy and self-enhancement are the reward. We grow through selfless loving, because sacrificial suffering sets us free to be more human and we are redeemed by it. The incense of a happy life arises only from the cinders of selfishness. A readiness to sacrifice ourselves, to transcend ourselves for others also enhances our own chances of survival in demanding situations. Asked how he endured the terrors of the Auschwitz death camp, one survivor told Viktor Frankl that he gave a small piece of his daily ration of hard brown bread to a fellow prisoner who was weaker than himself.

Sacrifice is a form of gift-giving, motivated by love. Rather than diminish us, it enhances our life through sharing it. It is useful to compare how we feel after a generous sacrificial act with how differently we feel after behaving selfishly. Which act brings the deeper feelings of satisfaction, joy and self-worth?

At the close of life, the question will not be 'How much have you gathered?' but 'How much have you given away?' It will not be 'How much have you won?' but 'How much have you done? It will not be 'How much have you saved for yourself?' but 'How much have you sacrificed for others?' Suffering and sacrifice are the other side of loving. Sharing the pain of the other and sometimes receiving pain from the other are part of loving. Sacrifice is the body language of love. Kahil Gibram has written: 'Out of suffering have emerged the strongest souls; the most massive characters are seared with scars.'

Just before his death in his lonely African clinic at Lambarene, Albert Schweitzer received a letter from the Austrian-born Israeli philosopher, Martin Buber, which contained this beautiful paragraph:

> Since my earliest years it has been a great encouragement, and in later years a comforting thought, that people like you exist. As you know, I have always been concerned with those who help mankind, and you have been one of the great helpers in so many ways. Every time one man helps another, the Hasidim [faithful Jews of the second century] say an angel is born. I hope that fate will long allow you to hear the wings of many angels beating about you.

The English word 'sacrifice' comes from the Latin words *sacrum facere*, 'to make sacred'. When selflessness, self-giving or sacrifice are involved, the action becomes sacred; it has transcended the merely human and touches on the divine within each of us.

# CHAPTER EIGHTEEN

# *Loved by God – Old Testament*

IT IS always interesting to see how different ethnic and cultural groups have tried to define love. Just like while gazing at the varied facets of a diamond there are many ways of looking at love. The aspect from which other persons or groups see and experience love makes it easier for us to know more of what love is. It will help us to look at the search of the Jewish people over centuries, for a description.

The prophet Jeremiah has God say to us, 'I have loved you with an everlasting love' (*Jeremiah* 31:3). The prophet Isaiah gives us the same message very visually when we hear God say, 'I have carved you on the palms of my hands' (*Isaiah* 49:16). Then God's love for us invites us to love one another, as when the prophet Micah asked us 'to act justly, love tenderly and walk humbly with your God' (*Micah* 6:8).

In the Old Testament, the first Covenant, whose sources date from the tenth to the sixth century BC, the authors use six Hebrew words to describe God's love for us. The study of each of these adds much to our modern understanding of the word 'love'.

*Da'ath* means the complete knowledge of each other when mutual love reaches near perfection. *Da'ath*-love presumes that, when sexual intimacy is honest and free, it is a total expression of mutual acceptance and of the appreciation that two people have for each other. It is often translated as *to know,* but the English word *know* does not express the inclusiveness and depth of *da'ath*. This word describes the intimacy of mutual self-revelation, of self-emptying and the deep loving which underlies total, truthful openness of people to each other. It expresses the beautiful gift of self and the joyful reception of two people who give themselves to each other totally.

Martha Nussbaum, Professor of Ethics in Chicago University, reminded us of a profound truth when she wrote: 'some forms of knowledge are available only through love'. *Da'ath* expresses what often happens in moments of silence between two people who love each other as they grow in mutual admiration and reverence together. It contains the sense of a reciprocal respectful exploration of each other's attractiveness that continues until death separates them. The author of Proverbs reminds us: 'the knowledge [*da'ath*] of the Holy One is insight' (*Proverbs* 9:10). *Da'ath*-love – God's love for us – says 'We are almost one'.

The word *'Emeth* means firm, faithful, reliable and lasting love. It expresses the reality of mutual trust that always accompanies true love. When *'emeth* is present, there is no distrust, no suspicion and no need for doubt or wariness between two people. The two people have total confidence in each other and do not feel that there is any risk in giving power or control to the other. Because there is *emeth* between them, there is a readiness to commit themselves to each other for ever. Each one knows that they can rely on the other, because the other is totally dependable. This relationship does not depend on law or duty, because it is spontaneous and always predictable. Each person has total faith in the other. Each can say about the other that their word is their bond and never in need of being investigated or questioned. The prophet Micah addresses God confidently: 'You will show faithfulness [*'emeth*] to Jacob and unswerving loyalty to Abraham, as you have sworn to our ancestors from the days of old (*Micah* 7:20).' *'Emeth*-love says,

'I trust you totally because I know you will never let me down.'

The word *chesed* is often translated as 'mercy', but it is deeper than this. It expresses the limitlessness of love. *Chesed* promises that love will never cease, never give up. The demands of expectancy, convention or duty do not put limits to *chesed* love. *Chesed* love is more than an act of mercy, it is a permanently merciful attitude of God's heart and implies a promise and a commitment to the other person, which will never be broken. *Chesed* love is fully reliable and is totally trustworthy. *Chesed* implies a willing bond, a freely given commitment to each other.

This commitment is given to a person who is known, not to a stranger. The word *chesed* is used to express, not merely the initial act of mutual commitment, but the ongoing actions that will be done for the other person. This love seeks out extra opportunities to help the other person, and to make them happier. It is the opposite of a legal marriage contract when the inadequacy, the weakness or the possible failure of love needs to be enshrined in law. It eliminates the possibility of naming any conditions before or during a marriage or in a relationship. The refrain of *Psalm* 136 is 'O give thanks to the Lord, for he is good, for his steadfast love [*chesed*] endures forever.' *Chesed*-love says, 'My love for you has no limits in action or in time, and your failure to love me does not change my enduring love for you'.

The word *Racham* is related to the Hebrew word for womb. It is a word that seeks to bring security to the life of another. It means a feeling of care, resulting in a readiness to help another person in need. More deeply, it is the capacity to feel the discomfort or pain of the other who may not be a friend but may be a stranger. The English word which expresses *racham* best is 'compassion'. As mentioned in Chapter Nine, 'To Love Is to Forgive', the Latin origin of the word *compassion* suggests suffering with another. For people whose emotional life is healthy, this feeling is instinctive. Parents especially experience *racham*. It describes the discomfort they feel even in their own bodies when one of their children is ill. *Racham* leads to a caring response for the other who is in need, or who is upset for whatever cause. It describes lives of long dedication in helping the poor, the sick or those marginalized in any way. The word *racham* says, 'I feel your pain or weakness, and I am willing to ease it'. This is God's love for us. The word 'mercy' is a close English equivalent. In Scripture, *racham* is not just how God responds to our pleadings for mercy, but it is God's permanent attitude before our failures. 'If you return to the Lord your God, and you and your children obey him with all your hearts and with all your soul … The Lord your God will restore your fortunes and have compassion [*racham*] on you.' (*Deuteronomy* 30:2-3). The word *racham* describes God's deep, merciful, compassionate, affectionate and tender womb-love for us.

The word *Chen* expresses the idea of giving a favour without any dependence on repayment in return. It is love given without reason. It comes simply from the goodness of the giver's heart. It is love offered solely from a generous heart on the part of the lover. It is kindness given without expecting any return. At the time that the word was first used, it was associated with the nobility or with a hospitable aristocracy. It expresses the idea of unmerited gift. The word 'grace' is a close English equivalent. The person who receives this kind of love is usually pleasantly surprised at the unexplained graciousness that is often called grace. *Chen* could be described as a rich overflow from a person already richly endowed with a loving heart. *Chen*-love says 'Please accept the surprise of my unconditional love for you'. In *Genesis* (33:5) we read: 'When Esau looked up, and saw the women and children, he said, "Who are these with you?" Jacob answered "these are the children whom God has graciously [*chen*] given your servant".' *Chen* describes God's astonishing, unearned love for us.

The word *'aheb* describes the love that selects one person from among and above others. It implies that a person has looked around, has met many others, and compared them with this new friend. As a result of this searching, two people decide to focus their love on each other in a unique way. It is much more than the act of pity or feeling sorry for the other, as these are feelings that can come from instinct alone. This heart-felt kindness for another is a recognition that this person is special. It is the 'I do' spoken in connection with marriage or the unspoken loyalty of any other deep friendship. It is commitment to care for the long term. This form of love involves continual forgiveness of the other. It is the most frequent word for love in the Hebrew Bible. In the book of *Genesis* (37:3) we read, 'Now Israel loved [*'aheb*] Joseph more than any other of his children because he was the son of his old age.' *'Aheb*-love says 'I love you enough to take wholehearted responsibility for your growth and welfare because you are special to me.'

Each of these words describes an aspect of love which most of us have experienced, and which we put into practice at some time in our lives. Occasionally we practise all of them at the same time, and most of us strive to practise them as often as we can. Many happily married and unmarried people live all of these aspects in their practice of love.

From time to time, people of deep faith experience God as loving them in all of these ways. When they are lovingly put into practice towards our neighbour, we can be sure that we are loving God, whether we are aware of it or not. While a person's love of

God does not depend entirely on church affiliation, full-hearted membership of the church community will always authenticate and enhance our relationship with God.

People of faith believe that God who is love has loved us, not only that we might love God in return, but so that we might return that divine love by loving one another, as St John reminds us: 'Beloved, let us love one another, because love is from God' (1 *John* 4:7). The Evangelical writer on spirituality, John Henry Jowett, puts it this way: 'God does not comfort us to make us comfortable but to make us comforters'. St John also assures us that 'a person who does not love his or her brother or sister whom they can see, cannot love God whom they have never seen' (1 *John* 4:20). Monk and mystic Thomas Merton has written: 'A man cannot enter into the deeper centre of himself and pass through that centre into God unless he is ready to pass entirely out of himself, empty himself and give himself to others in the purity of selfless love'. Protestant theologian Karl Barth wrote: 'Meet the world with the fullness of your being and you shall meet God. If you wish to believe, love.'

Whether we are aware of it or not, any authentic friendship mediates God to us if we are open to receive the divine presence. In our everyday lives, God's face is clearest to us in friendship. As we touch our friends in any of these six ways in human loving, we are like blind people tracing with tentative fingers the unseen features of the face of God.

# CHAPTER NINETEEN

# Loved by God – New Testament

THEOLOGIAN Karl Rahner wrote: 'Christianity is not a religion that solves all the riddles of the universe, but one that
gives us the courage, by the grace of God, to shelter oneself in
an incomprehensible mystery and to believe that this mystery
is love'.

The word 'mystery' in Scripture means something so deep
that it is endlessly rich. All love is mystery in this sense. Nevertheless, it can help our hearts to respond when we think about
the meaning of love, as we have throughout this book. Now I
invite you, the reader, to think about the love God has for us,
as described in the New Testament.

## GOD FEELS WITH US

All love begins when we try to feel with others and, as far as
possible, to identify with their feelings, as we saw in Chapter
Five. It is easy sometimes to sense that the infinite God does not
feel our joys, sorrows, fears, hopes and our need for friendship.
The New Testament assures us otherwise. The first chapter of
St John's Gospel tells us that God became human, and in the
Letter to the Hebrews we are assured that he became like his
brothers and sisters in every respect except in sin. Jesus even
experienced sin in some mysterious way, as Paul told the Corinthians, 'For our sake God made him to be sin who knew no
sin' (2 *Corinthians* 5:21). We are also assured that although he
did not sin, in his fullness of humanity 'in every respect [he]
has been tested as we are' (*Hebrews* 4:15).

The four Gospels record that, in his life of love for us, Jesus shared our experiences and that he felt most of our human feelings. Like all of us, after nine months in his mother's womb, he was born as we were. 'He grew in wisdom, age and grace' and we are told that he played games with other children. Every Jewish child's education consisted in studying the Scriptures and learning a trade. His listeners called him 'the carpenter, the son of Mary'. At times he was tired and hungry, and on one occasion he fell asleep on a boat during a storm. At other times his friends gave a banquet for him. Luke tells us that at least on one occasion 'they laughed at him'. He enjoyed the company of little children, and he rebuked his apostles when they tried to send their mothers away. He expressed anger when the Temple was being used by unjust traders, and again when the priests were failing to care for the people. Jesus had women companions who accompanied him and who stood by his cross when all but one of his apostles deserted him. Martha and Mary offered him special hospitality in their home. Having cured a little girl, he took her by the hand and told her family to give her something to eat.

Like us, he felt the burdens of being human when he was hungry, thirsty, tired or annoyed. He was hurt when one of his apostles sold him, when another denied knowing him, and when nine of them deserted him, but he was delighted when a Roman army officer expressed faith in him. He dreaded pain and he asked God to take it away. Twice he asked God to release him from his given mission, and on the cross he even felt doubt about God's care for him, just as we sometimes do. He defended an adulterous woman, and with his last breath he asked his mother and John to take care of each other.

Each of these incidents shows us that we have a God who

has chosen to accompany us and to feel with us on our human journey.

### GOD ACCEPTS US WHERE WE ARE 'AT'

Jesus took the second step in loving us by accepting us as we are and where we are on our journey. We recall Zacchaeus, the despised tax collector. As such, Zacchaeus was designated a sinner and a totally marginalized person in his community because he had identified himself with the Romans and forced taxes from his own people. His curiosity and his fear of being lynched drove him to climb a tree to see Jesus. In love, Jesus called him down, but fear deterred him until Jesus told him to hurry down so that they could share a meal together. Jesus did not mention his sinfulness nor did he ask him for a promise not to sin again before having a meal in friendship with him. Jesus fully accepted Zacchaeus just as he was; he offered him friendship from where he was 'at'.

This is how God loves us; he continues to offer us his love and friendship no matter how we have failed. God's love for us is not less when we sin. His infinite love for us is stable, irreversible and unchanging. His loving acceptance of us does not depend on the rightness of our behaviour. God cannot love us more if we pray more or if we behave better, because he cannot increase or decrease what he is. St John assures us: 'God is love'. God condemns sin but he never condemns the sinner.

### GOD'S LOVE ENCOURAGES US TO GROW

While we are assured in Scripture (*Hebrews* 4:15 and 5:2) that we have in Christ a high priest who is able to sympathize with our weakness, and who is able to deal gently with us when we are ignorant and have gone astray, our God wants us to grow.

While God accepts us as we are, he continues to call us forward. There is a divine desire that we continue to grow in every way. Like the love of devoted parents, God's love intensely desires us to grow in beauty and goodness. God does not want us to stagnate in our development in any way.

The author of the *Letter to the Ephesians* put it this way: 'Be imitators of God, as beloved children, and live in love, as Christ loved us'. God calls us forward in our growth; his love for us encourages us to develop, to become our best selves. In Matthew's Gospel, we are reminded to develop our talents, not to hoard or to hide them. Growth is a frequent theme in the Christian life. The Ephesians are encouraged to grow and to further the growth of the Church community: 'We must grow up in every way into him who is the head, into Christ, from whom the whole body, joined and knitted together by every ligament with which it is equipped, as each part is working properly, promotes the body's growth in building itself up in love' (*Ephesians* 4:15-16). To the Colossian community, St Paul speaks about 'a growth that is from God' (*Colossian* 2:19). In his briefest statement telling us why he came on earth, Jesus said 'I came that they may have life, and have it abundantly' (*John* 10:10).

### GOD HELPS US

God helps us when he speaks to us through the Holy Spirit living in our hearts, when his voice guides us to do what is best for our own welfare. This is God's primary way to help us. It is only in prayerful listening and discernment that we can hear this precious message. 'I will ask the Father, and he will give you another Advocate, to be with you for ever. This is the Spirit of truth, whom the world cannot receive, because it neither sees him nor knows him. You know him, because he abides with you, and he will be in in you' (*John* 14:16-17). He gives us total freedom while at the same time offering us his guidance which we must discern carefully amidst all the other voices within and around us

We know that God always helps us in the struggles of our daily lives. He does so through others, by asking everyone who knows us to help us by their prayers and practical action. God regards as done to himself everything that others do for us and to us. It is clear from this message that God has chosen to depend on the generosity of others to pass on his practical love to us. Loving parents are the first people through whom God helps us. Later, God helps us through our family, our friends and sometimes even through strangers. God acts to help us through the care of medical staff and through competent counsellors when we need them. Of course God always leaves us free to avail ourselves of divine help or not.

Jesus chose to give his apostles a vivid demonstration of how he wants others to help us when he poured water into a basin and washed his apostles' feet. Having done it, he said: 'You also ought to wash one another's feet. For I have set you an example, that you also should do as I have done to you' (*John* 13:14). This is always how God helps us. Miracles are very rare.

It is true that our faith is often tested by the apparent absence of God. His help does not always come in the way or at the time we expect it. God's love calls us to trust as Jesus did when he doubted his Father's help and cried out on the cross: 'My God, my God, why have you forsaken me?' God remained silent. Only the Holy Spirit in his heart enabled him to say in trust: 'Into your hands I commend my spirit.' Without removing the source of our stress or pain, God often gives us the strength to endure it, thus enabling us to say with St Paul:

Who will separate us from the love of Christ? Will hardship or distress, or persecution or famine or nakedness or peril or sword? In all these things we are more than conquerors through him who loved us. For I am convinced that neither death, nor life, nor angels, nor rulers, nor things present nor things to come, nor powers, nor height, nor depth nor anything else in all creation will be able to separate us from the love of God in Christ Jesus our Lord. (*Romans* 8:35-39)

### GOD FORGIVES US

God's love for us is always a forgiving love. In the Letter to the Hebrews, God assures us that we have a high priest who is able to sympathize with our weakness, and the writer continues: 'Let us therefore approach this throne of grace with boldness, so that we may receive mercy and find grace to help us in time of need' (*Hebrews* 4:16). God's forgiveness is waiting to pour over us when we acknowledge that we have sinned. We release God's abiding mercy when we confess our sins sincerely.

The story we have heard so often about the merciful father who forgave his selfish and wayward son is the perfect example of God's forgiving love. The boy returned to his home only because he was starving. His loving father, while enduring the pain of personal loss for many years, awaited his son's return. At the first sight of his ragged, shoeless boy, the father ran to meet him with the same love that he had in his heart before and since his boy had departed. The father was never angry nor offended; his only feeling was one of great sadness at his son's departure from the safety of his home. He did not ask the boy to name his sins in detail or to promise never to sin again.

There were no questions, no examinations of conscience, no remonstrations, no penance and no conditions set for the boy's return. The son had acknowledged his mistake when he said, 'I have sinned against heaven and before you' and that was sufficient. Sins acknowledged are sins forgiven. God assures us of this through St John: 'If we confess our sins, he who is faithful will forgive us our sins and cleanse us from all unrighteousness' (1 *John* 1:9).

### GOD INVITES US TO CELEBRATE

Our parents' love is always a source of conscious or subconscious celebration from our childhood into adulthood. We knew that we belonged. Those of us who were blessed with loving parents can appreciate these words of St John:

> See what love the Father has given us, that we should be called children of God; and that is what we are.... Beloved, we are children of God now; what we will be has not yet been revealed. What we do know is this, when he is revealed, we will be like him, for we will see him as he is. (1 *John* 3:1-2)

People who love and those who are loved live with a constant feeling of celebration despite the painful or difficult moments in their lives. In the Gospel story, the father who was so generous in his loving asked only that his son celebrate at a banquet with music and dancing to rejoice in his return. This image paints a beautiful picture of God's loving heart before our failures and repentance every day.

The choice to be together at a meal usually indicates friendship, and we often plan a meal to celebrate special shared occasions. This celebration is what took place at the Last Supper and can still take place each time we join in a Eucharist with our fellow Christians. Before that last meal, Jesus said to those around him: 'As the Father has loved me, so I have loved you; abide in my love ... I have said these things to you, so that my joy may be in you, and that your joy may be complete.' (*John* 5:9-10) God wants his love to be a source of joy, and an experience to be celebrated.

# CHAPTER TWENTY

# *Loving Others in God*

IF YOU are a disciple of Jesus you will know that, in his message recorded in the New Testament, faith and love are so linked as to be inseparable. St Paul expressed the link between faith and love in these words to the community at Galatia: 'The only thing that counts is faith working through love' (*Galatians* 5:6). This is also clear in St John's words: 'Those who do not love a brother or sister whom they have seen, cannot love God whom they have not seen.' We reach union with God through loving others.

On one occasion, at the request of a scribe, Jesus quoted the Old Testament commanding his people to love God and their neighbour, but there is no New Testament commandment which states that we must love God. Instead of saying that because God loved us we ought to love God, St John says: 'Since God loved us so much, we ought to love one another.' He continues: 'No one has ever seen God; if we love one another God lives in us and his love is perfected in us' (1 *John* 4:12). God wishes his great love for us to be returned to him through loving our neighbour.

For the believer, to love is not just a commandment, it is a gift of gentle energy received through faith, a gift given, and an experience to be passed on. St John puts it simply: 'We love because he first loved us' (1 *John* 4:19). God's gift of love is not just *to* us. It is meant to pass *through* us to others. We are privileged to be channels of God's love to the world. St John encourages us: 'My dear friends, let us love one another, since love comes from God; everyone who loves is born of God and knows God. Whoever does not love, does not know God, because God is love' (1 *John* 4:8).

During his final exhortation to his apostles, Jesus said: 'I give you a new commandment: 'Love one another as I have loved you' (*John* 13:34). The experience of being loved unconditionally by God is the standard and the motive of our love for one another. This is a much higher standard than the Old Testament command, 'Love your neighbour as yourself.'

The believer then is not someone who merely remembers, or who follows, imitates, obeys, adores Christ, or one who loves others in order to get to heaven. By faith and the presence of Christ's Spirit in his or her heart, the believer is now identified with Jesus Christ and is filled with his love. At his Last Supper, Jesus spoke to his Father about us: 'The glory that you have given me, I have given to them, so that they may be one as we are one, I in them and you in me, that they may become completely one, so that the world may know that you have sent me, and have loved them even as you have loved me.' In another part of that same prayer, he spoke to his Father, asking him that 'the love with which you loved me may be in them and that I too may be in them' (*John* 17.26). St Peter spoke to us of this great privilege, reminding us that we are already 'participants of the divine nature' (2 *Peter* 1:4), which is love. It is this divine love flowing into us which enables us to love one another as God loves us.

For the believer, love is not merely a commandment or a tiring effort; it is a power and an energy within us. Paul reminds us of this fact when he says that 'God's love has been poured into us through the Holy Spirit that has been given to us' (*Romans* 5:5). The word 'poured' is a translation of the Greek word *encheo*, which expresses the idea of something poured lavishly. God's love is being poured into our hearts so that it may be poured out on everyone we meet. Consequently, we love one another, not merely by imitating Christ's love, but by allowing him to pour his love abundantly through us into others. All believers' love is divine love flowing copiously from their hearts to others.

For those who have faith, loving others is not just a series of disconnected acts but is a way of life, sustaining and expressing the believer's union with God. It is because God made us to receive and to give love that we have loving hearts which create an attitude, an outlook, a disposition to love. There exists in each of us the possibility of a positive approach to all other people, no matter how they treat us. St John identifies this truthful and loving attitude when he says that he hopes his community is 'walking in the truth' and 'walking in love'.

Jesus' statement of why he had come among us includes these words: 'The Spirit of the Lord is upon me, because he has anointed me to bring good news to the poor. He sent me to proclaim release to the captives and recovery of sight to the blind and to let the oppressed go free.' (*Luke* 4:18). Each one of us is impoverished in some way because we remain deprived of full physical, emotional, mental or moral well-being. We all need to be constantly enriched, to be helped in some aspects of our lives and to hear good news regularly. We need to be released from the captivity of our inherited deprivations, from the results of some parental failures in early life, from minor or serious illnesses, from temperamental biases, from tendencies towards selfishness and often from our silence about social injustice in systems around us. Everyone needs to be freed from these limitations so that we can love more fully and act more generously. In this deep sense we are all poor.

There are moments of blindness in each of our lives when we fail to see or choose not to see what might be good for us or for others. Each of us can feel burdened in some way by personal weakness in the face of the struggles of life. Many people feel oppressed by the misuse of power in society and in the church. Here too we all need to receive the good news of loving assistance from one another.

These poverties, these needs for support in ourselves and in others present us with opportunities to accept love and to give love. We know that God has gifted each of us in unique ways, and Jesus reminds us that these talents were not given to be wrapped up and put away safely, or to be used in caring only for ourselves. They are given so that we can express our love in helping others as St Peter exhorts us to do: 'Like good stewards of the manifold grace of God, serve one another with whatever gift each of you has received' (1 *Peter* 4:10).

St James reminds us that our service of others must be practical: 'If good deeds do not go with faith, it is quite dead' (*James* 2:14), and the New Testament gives us examples of these good deeds by which we can pass God's good news on to one another.

Carry each other's burdens (*Galatians* 6:2)

Have a tender heart and a humble mind (1 *Peter* 3:8)

Wash one another's feet (*John* 13:14)

Extend hospitality to strangers (*Romans* 12:13)

Admonish one another in all wisdom (*Colossians* 3:16)

Do not repay evil for evil, abuse for abuse (1 *Peter* 3:9)

Encourage and build each other up (1 *Thessalonians* 5:11)

With patience, bear with one another in love (*Ephesians* 4:2)

Teach and admonish one another (*Colossians* 3:16)

Balance your abundance with other's need (2 *Corinthians* 8:14)

Have unity of Spirit among you (1 *Peter* 3:8)

Always seek to do good to one another (1 *Thessalonians* 5:15)

Put up with the failings of the weak (*Romans* 15:1)

Be compassionate, kind, meek and patient (*Colossians* 3:12)

I was naked and you clothed me (*Matthew* 25:36)

Love one another deeply from the heart (1 *Peter* 1:22)

Sell your possessions and give alms (*Luke* 13:33)

Be clothed with compassion and kindness (*Colossians* 3:12)

Bless those who persecute you (*Romans* 12:14)

Do not be haughty. Associate with the lowly (*Romans* 12:16)

Weep with those who weep (*Romans* 12:15)

Encourage the faint-hearted, help the weak (1 *Thessalonians* 5:14)

Forgive as the Lord has forgiven you (*Colossians* 3:13)

Provoke one another to love and good works (*Hebrews* 10:24)

I was hungry and you gave me to eat (*Matthew* 25:35)

No bitterness, anger, wrangling and slander (*Ephesians* 4:31)

Rejoice with those who rejoice (*Romans* 12:15)

Welcome others as Christ welcomed you (*Romans* 15:7)

Do not judge or condemn others (*Luke* 6:37)

Put yourselves at the service of others (1 *Corinthians* 16:16)

Be humble, gentle and patient (*Ephesians* 4:2)

Have sympathy and love for one another (1 *Peter* 3:8)

Do not seek your own advantage (1 *Corinthians* 10:33)

Love one another with mutual affection (*Romans* 12:10)

I was sick and you cared for me (*Matthew* 25:36)

I was in prison and you visited me (*Matthew* 25:36)

Contribute to each other's needs (*Romans* 12:13)

If your enemies are hungry, feed them (*Romans* 12:20)

Live in harmony with one another (*Romans* 12:16)

Be generous and ready to share (1 *Timothy* 6:18)

Bear with one another in love (*Ephesians* 4:2)

Lay down your lives for one another (1 *John* 3:16)

Live in love, as Christ loved you (*Ephesians* 5:2)

In practising these calls to love, we respond to St John's appeal: 'Little children, let us love, not in word or speech, but in truth and action' (1 *John* 3:18). The down-to-earth nature of these texts confirms what St Teresa wrote: 'We cannot know whether or not we love God, but there can be no doubt about whether or not we love our neighbour.' Neighbour-love is very visible when it is present, and very noticeable when it is absent.

This frequent invitation to reach out and to accept the privilege of loving others is also expressed by St Paul when we read: 'If I speak with the tongues of mortals and of angels, but have not love, I am a noisy gong or a clanging cymbal.... If I give away all my possessions, but do not have love, I am nothing' (1 *Corinthians* 13). We also read: 'Those who do not love a brother or sister whom they have seen cannot love God whom they have not seen' (1 *John* 4:20); and 'If I have all faith so as to remove mountains, but have not love, I am nothing' (1 *Corinthians* 13:2). Most of us are familiar with this description of love by St Paul:

> Love is patient; love is kind; love is not envious or boastful or arrogant or rude. It does not insist on its own way; it is not irritable or resentful; it does not rejoice in wrongdoing but rejoices in the truth. It bears all things, hopes all things, endures all things. Love never ends. (1 *Corinthians* 13:4-8)

The following is a rhymed statement of what is in this chapter:

> I sought to find the will of God.
> I climbed the nearest steeple.
> But God said, 'climb down, my friend'.
> I am found among the people.

Poet, painter, engraver and mystic, William Blake wrote:

I sought my soul but my soul I could not see.
I sought my God but my God eluded me.
I sought my neighbour and I found all three.

# CHAPTER TWENTY-ONE

# *Loving the Unloved*

SIXTY-TWO years ago, in his book *The Sane Society*, Erich Fromm wrote: 'Love is not primarily a relationship to a specific person; it is an attitude, an ordination of character which determines the relatedness of the person to the world as a whole, not towards one object of love'. He also wrote: 'One cannot be responsive to the world without being responsible. If a person loves only one other person and is indifferent to all others, his love is not love but a symbiotic attachment (*i.e.*, selfish co-dependency), or an enlarged egoism'.

It may seem strange but it is true that those who need love most are the people we know least. Those most in need of love are on the margins of society and of society's consciousness. It may be that their unusually high need for love is the very reason why they are beyond our awareness. It may be that our culture is gradually teaching us to build walls around us, or to pull down blinds to protect us from seeing those who are suffering. Yet by becoming human God gave a new value, a divine dignity to every man, woman and child. As believers, none of us can deliberately keep anyone on the margin of our consciousness. When the pain of the world enters into our consciousness we cannot help feeling powerless, sad, even angry and somewhat isolated in our world today.

In 2016, the United Nations' reports tell us that two billion of the world's 7.3 billion people did not have enough to eat, and that 650 million families have been forced to flee from their homes. At present there are 65 million migrants, half of whom are children. These reports also tell us that 18 million children are forced to work in partial or total slavery. Unless they are living close to us, the materially poor, the hungry, the homeless, the friendless, the excluded, the lonely, the mentally ill, the imprisoned, and those dying alone sometimes do not reach our awareness. The despairing, the enslaved, the trafficked, the suicidal, those trapped in brothels and those forced to drink polluted water perhaps do not disturb us enough to act for their welfare. Those living under tyranny, the silenced, the tortured and the anxious mothers tempted to abort their babies need to remain in our consciousness. Though there is sometimes little we as individuals can do directly to help these suffering people, we can take the first step in loving them by being aware of them and by encouraging friends to do likewise. We can then hope that some action will follow.

Closer to home, many very lonely people remain unvisited in comfortable hospitals and retirement homes. These people are in great need of being loved, but for most of us they are somehow far away. They seem to be, and sometimes are, out of our reach. Most of them live on the painful perimeter of society despite the efforts of many voluntary groups to help them.

It is good to ask ourselves, from time to time, how many prisoners of conscience, how many refugees, how many of the exploited, how many illiterate, how many unemployed, how many overworked and how many people with special needs feel that we are on their side? How many broken families, how many abused children, how many young widows and widowers, how many permanently ill or how many, whose lives are empty of meaning, am I ever in contact with?

There are many excellent organizations working to help these neglected individuals. Yet much social work is for a purpose, while loving must always be for the person. Those being helped easily sense the difference. Despite the professional activity of social workers, many of these people still feel on the margin and unloved.

On another level, there are many rich people whose wealth possesses them, whose money marginalizes them from the poor. There are many people whose avaricious lives are deprived of any spiritual dimension. There are many well-off people suffering from endless restlessness as they anxiously search the fluctuations of the stock market every morning. Jesus reminds us that those who 'pull down their barns to build bigger ones' (*Luke* 12:18) have chosen to live outside the salvation he offers. There are many people who are exhausted trying desperately to fill the emptiness within them by some form of addiction. Many rich people can be very poor in what ultimately satisfies the human heart. Sadly, and through no fault of their own, there are many guilt-ridden, church-going people whose lives lack authentic spirituality and who fail to find love, even in the Christian community.

All of these unloved people live stressful and pain-filled lives. Deep down they feel deprived and on the margin of communities. They are known and named only as members of the group that suffers the same deprivation. Do we feel compassion for them? Do we love them enough to pray for them when we cannot help them in any other way?

On his first visit to the local synagogue, the scroll of the prophet Isaiah was given to Jesus to read and to speak about. He chose to unroll it at these words: 'The Spirit of the Lord is upon me, because he has anointed me to bring good news to the poor. He has sent me to proclaim release to the captives and recovery of sight to the blind, and to let the oppressed go free and to proclaim the year of the Lord's favour.' Then he sat down and said: 'Today this scripture has been fulfilled in your hearing' (*Luke* 4:18-21). This was Jesus' policy speech telling God's people why he had come on earth: to love especially those who were on the margins and who were neglected by society and by their religious leaders.

These people were either foreign-born or were Samaritans, prostitutes, lepers, the blind, the lame or the tax collectors. To a certain extent all women were also marginalized. Jesus agreed with the prophet Isaiah that these rejected people, who the leaders referred to as sinners, were the poor, the captives, the blind and the oppressed. On another occasion he spoke of those who were poor, hungry, sad, hated, excluded, reviled and defamed, and he called them blessed. He had come to establish a community - his apostles, his disciples, his church who would manifestly love the marginalized. He healed the lepers, he gave sight to the blind, he cured the lame and made the deaf hear. He expected his followers to mediate God's love and to care for all those who were neglected, as he had done. Today, as in the past, many skilled people, young and old, leave their homeland to serve in developing countries. With Jesus these generous people are saying: 'Come to me you who are weary and are carrying heavy burdens, and I will give you rest.' (*Matthew* 11:28).

Many voluntary service agencies and social justice movements work locally to help the neglected in our society. It may be possible to join one of these groups or to support their work in whatever way we can. St John identifies our sharing with others with our love for God in these words: 'How does the love of God abide in anyone who has the world's goods and sees a brother or sister in need, yet refuses to help?' (1 *John* 3:17)

Justice usually means doing the right thing according to a

moral code such as paying just wages, but biblical justice is much deeper and more demanding. Justice in the Scriptures means fidelity to the relationships between God and us and between one another. It is founded on the presence of God in one another and on mutual respect for the dignity of each person. It is expressed in the duty and privilege of actively supporting one another and of building up one another. We do not really understand social justice or believe in it fully until we are, in some way, lovingly involved with those who are struggling on the margins of society.

This involvement can take many forms because it depends on our individual circumstances. These include our health, age, family commitments and freedom from other loving activities with those close to us. At times, our only involvement might be words of encouragement or our constant prayer for the welfare of any neglected people.

Anything we can say or do to improve human rights, to alleviate malnourishment, to safeguard adequate health care for all, to assure social security in times of sickness or in old age, to improve the disparity between rich and poor is active love of others. To help improve immigration policies, to ensure equitable global trade, or to prevent climate chaos is to love people we may never know. Any action to help lessen crime and corruption is also showing love for our fellow human beings. Our individual willingness to live a less luxurious lifestyle and to share generously, confirms and encourages those who are more directly involved in social justice leadership. In this way we can join Jesus and say: 'The Spirit of the Lord is upon me, because he has anointed me to bring good news to the poor, to proclaim release to captives, and to let the oppressed go free' (*Luke* 4.18). These words were first spoken by the prophet Isaiah around 520

BC. He was direct and uncompromising in condemning social injustice and false worship. To people who practised fasting but who were unjust to others, Isaiah has God say:

> Is not this the fast that I choose: to loose the bonds of injustice, to undo the thongs of the yoke, to let the oppressed go free, and to break every yoke. Is it not to share your bread with the hungry, and bring the homeless into your house, and when you see the naked to cover them (*Isaiah* 58:6).

Most believers recite the Our Father every day. In it we say, 'Thy kingdom come'. This kingdom or reign of God already exists in heaven. We pray that it will come on earth. St Paul describes this kingdom. It is where 'righteousness, peace and joy' are abundant among people in every city, town, village, community and family. Righteousness exists when people live together in a way that is morally right, just and loving. Peace exists where there is harmony in people's hearts and among them. Joy follows peace because then there are reasons for satisfaction and celebration in communities. The world, at present, is far from this ideal situation but we must continue our work to grow towards it.

All this is common sense but it is also the presence of God in people's hearts and among them. It is the victory of selflessness over selfishness, of gentleness over violence, of patience over impatience, of kindness over cruelty, of generosity over avarice, of self-control over impulsivity and of love over hate or disinterest. The phrase 'Kingdom of God' is the most repeated phrase in the four Gospels. It means a love-inspired, God-aided transformation of self and of the world.

In the synod document *Justice in the World* (1977), Church

teaching emphasised that 'Christian love of neighbour and the practice of justice cannot be separated. Love implies an absolute demand for justice, namely a recognition of the dignity and rights of one's neighbour. Because everyone is a true image of the invisible God, a brother or sister of Christ, the Christian finds God himself and God's absolute demand for justice and love in every man and woman.

The words of Pope Francis, spoken in February 2015 to the newly appointed cardinals, are important for all of us:

> I urge you to serve the Church in such a way that Christians will not be tempted to turn to Jesus without turning to the outcast. I urge you to seek the Lord in every excluded person who is hungry, thirsty or naked and to see the Lord who is imprisoned, sick, unemployed, persecuted. I urge you to seek the Lord in the leper, whether in body or soul, who encounters discrimination! We will not find the Lord unless we seek him in the marginalized.

To encourage us in our efforts, it is worth noting that *The Economist* (1 April 2017) quoting the World Bank, tells us that in 1981, some 42% of the world's population had barely enough to eat or of other necessities. Many were starving. But in 2013, just 10.7% of the world's population was similarly destitute. Poverty has almost certainly retreated further since 2013 and the Brookings Institution calculates that one person in our world now escapes extreme poverty every 1.2 seconds.

# CHAPTER TWENTY-TWO

# Loving Our Shared Home

HOME is a place where life is shared. Whatever happens to a *house* which shelters *a home* affects all of the people living in it. When one person makes the home a safer or more comfortable place, all the others feel the benefit. Care taken in a home by one member is love given to the others, and when the house is damaged by one person, it is a failure to love the others. If someone puts a hole in the roof or damages the heating system, everyone suffers, just as all benefit when the plumbing or the painting is improved.

Planet Earth is our shared home. Each member of the human family has responsibility for its well-being. None of us wants to flood people or other species from their homes or set fire to forests where they live or destroy their health by poisoning the air that they breathe. In our hearts most of us desire that every person be safe and comfortable in their homes and in their communities. In our behaviour, however, we need to be much more sensitive in carrying out the desires of our hearts. We must become more aware that what we do to the Earth can influence the welfare of all its inhabitants. How we act towards our environment now is a measure of our love for the whole community of creation living on planet Earth and for the generations to come. The hope is that, in caring for our common home, all people and every species will feel more at home in our common home.

Our shared home, the known universe, has a great prehistory that we can trace back 13.7 billion years. What we call our universe began in what is popularly called the Big Bang, an explosion of energy that contained all the light and energy we ever had, have now and will have in the future. The Big Bang is the source of everything that exists, even of our bodies in which our souls dwell. And we do not know what, if anything, existed before it.

One billion years after that great flaring forth, a combination of dust and expanding energy led to the formation of an endless number of stars. Then, by the power of gravity, the stars came together in clusters that we call galaxies. There are billions of these galaxies in our universe with billions of stars in each.

One of these star-filled galaxies which we call the Milky Way came into existence over 12 billion years ago. The Sun is one of its stars which came to birth around 5 billion years ago. Around it, eight known planets orbit, one of which we call planet Earth. It orbits the Sun at 1,000 miles an hour. There was no life on it until about 3.5 billion years ago when elementary life began to form deep within the ancient seas. Then, around 425 million years ago this life crawled out of the seas and appeared on earth in very primitive forms. Later, this primitive life evolved into plants, reptiles, insects, birds, animals and mammals. Despite continuing extensive research, no life has so far been found anywhere else in the universe.

About 2.6 million years ago, a type of human with brains and a nervous system developed on the earth. But it was only 128,000 years ago, when everything time-wise and distance-wise from the Sun and from the other planets was suitable for our emergence, that we modern humans evolved. The slightest change in evolution along the journey from the Big Bang would have made this emergence of the human species impossible. After billions of years in preparation, the universe welcomed us into its expanding embrace, and it has sustained us there ever since. The physicist, Freeman Dyson, who won the Templeton Prize in 2000, wrote: 'The universe knew we were coming.' Our present position and our journey around the Sun are also perfect for our continued survival.

The evolution and growth of our bodies are connected with everything that happened right back to the Big Bang; our bodies are part of the dust of the galaxies and of the slime of the seas. So too, every fish, insect, bird, animal and living thing comes from the same source. Every person and every pebble carries the history of everything that happened from the beginning. No person can choose not to be connected, because everything and every living body has some of the same 92 basic elements.

In her wonderful book, *Out of Wonder: The Evolving Story of the Universe*, Nellie McLaughlin reminds us that we are situated in a web of life, and that 'the same currents that run through our human blood also run through the swirling galaxies and through the myriad life forms that pervade our planet'. The slightest change in any part of this dynamically linked-up universe affects every other part of it, however slightly. The movement of a bird's wing influences the stars, and all human activity influences everything else in the cosmos. Every harmful act damages all creation in some way and every caring action has a positive effect on it.

Of everything that evolved since the Big Bang we humans are unique because we have self-reflective consciousness. We are the universe looking at itself and reflecting on its self. Dogs can be our 'friends', dolphins can imitate us, whales can sing, elephants can recall past sadness, and parrots can copy our speech. We share 96% of our DNA with our nearest known relatives. Animals and other species seem to have some emotional intelligence but we, and we alone, as far as is currently known, are the consciousness of everything that exists. With our arrival the universe became conscious of itself for the first time. We are embodied beings who know that we know, and who are aware that we are aware.

Charles Darwin in his *Origin of Species* wrote: 'There is a grandeur in this view of life, with its many powers having been breathed by the creator into new forms or into one. This planet has gone circling on according to the fixed law of gravity from so simple a beginning, and endless forms most beautiful and most wonderful have been and are being evolved.'

It helps to reflect on the miracle of our existence in such an awesome universe. Francis S. Collins, the geneticist behind the Human Genome Project, wrote: 'At the most fundamental level, it's a miracle that there is a universe at all. It's a miracle that it has order, fine-tuning that allows the possibility of complexity and laws that follow precise mathematical formulas. There must be a mind behind all this. To me, it qualifies as a miracle, a profound truth that lies outside scientific explanation.'

In recent years we humans, particularly in the so-called Western world, are seriously upsetting the harmony of our planet and our own existence in it. Through irresponsible behaviour we have reached a threshold which is endangering the diversity of life on Earth. By causing climate chaos we are ravaging the world that welcomed us.

This abuse of our shared home reflects our ignorance, selfishness, ingratitude, our lack of compassion, and our failure to love and respect the gift of a universe that supports us. In European countries, we no longer see as many birds, bees, butterflies, insects or worms as we did in the past. Mass extinctions took place when planets collided and the dinosaurs were killed, but today humans are continuously contributing to the extinctions of animals and plants by causing climate chaos. Animals are becoming extinct at a faster rate than ever before. In her comprehensive book, *Ask the Beasts*, Elizabeth Johnson reminds us that the United Nations Environmental Programme warns us that, in contrast to the normal rate of extinction which is one species every year, 150 to 200 now become extinct every day.

Climate change hurts the poorest countries most. At the present moment more than two billion people lack access to safe clean water, and larger numbers lack adequate nourishment, despite the massive waste of good food and clean water in developed countries. As the melting of Arctic glaciers increases, the ocean levels continue to rise throughout the world. Due to rising sea levels, some small island countries, such as Vanuatu, Kiribati and Tuvalu may soon disappear entirely beneath rising seas. In Bangladesh, 40 million people live just one metre above present sea level. Due to excessive rainfall, topsoil, which is vital for growth, is lessening seriously in Malta, the Philippines and Haiti. In their common letter, Pope Francis and Patriarch Kirill wrote, 'Unrelenting consumerism in some more developed countries is gradually depleting the resources of our planet'. In his encyclical letter *Laudato Si'* Pope Francis gives us encompassing motives and important ways to care for the Earth.

Before we take steps to prevent any further climate chaos, our attitudes before everything in our planet must change to one of love and respect. Then love of our shared home will change our consumerist behaviour and make us call for better leadership from those with political power. Only when we develop a deeper sense of loving admiration for the miracle of sunrises and sunsets, of starlit skies, of beautiful scenery and of all life that sustains us, will we be inspired to act generously to save the universe. At the same time, we can encourage others to join us. We must all endeavour to hear the cry of our damaged Earth, and to start healing the harm already done. By feeling the pain of our hurting environment and by growing in compassion for our fellow beings, we will endeavour to do all we can for the future health of our planet and its people. Time is running out; many experts claim that we are the last generation whose actions can act to keep our planet a place for living organisms to survive and to flourish.

There are encouraging signs in that many people are beginning to feel the pain of the world as their own pain, many who are growing in their awareness of the harm already done. As a leader in the Catholic Ecological Movement, Thomas Berry, wrote, 'Planet and people go into the future together or not at all', and Ban Ki Moon, former secretary general of the United Nations, reminded us there is no plan B because there is no planet B. There is a growing awareness that we have been given our world not only for our own enjoyment but also to pass it on lovingly to our children. What kind of world do we wish to pass on to them? Will they thank us or blame us?

St Thomas Aquinas wrote: 'The immense diversity and pluriformity of creation represents God more perfectly than any one creature alone. The destruction of any part of creation, especially the extinction of species, defaces the image of God that is etched in creation.' And poet Robert Browning wrote: 'God is the perfect poet, who speaks in his own creation.'

What can we do to help? One formula being offered to keep us in harmony with our shared home is:

Respect the environment and everything in it.

Reduce our consumption of all food, especially meat.

Repair rather than replace with the new, where possible.

Recycle rather than discard as much as we can of our waste.

Reducing our use of coal, oil, gas, bog turf, diesel, petrol and electricity would be a good start in lowering $CO_2$ omissions. By setting a washing machine to wash at lower temperatures or by turning hot-water taps off when not in use, by taking a shower instead of a bath, we can save hundreds of pounds of $CO_2$. Energy-efficient refrigerators can do the same. Using our cars less by car-sharing or by cycling is a real contribution. Insulating our homes would help greatly in saving the Earth's energy. Solar panels are also notable energy savers. Planting native trees and flowers that pollinate helps to save the bees whose continued existence is so important to our welfare.

The overarching urgency for us humans is to re-connect with our deepest roots, the world of nature. We need to spend more time communing with nature in the knowledge that God is present in every atom and aspect of creation – ourselves and the whole community of life.

It is important to accept that if we harm our environment we are guilty, and to recognize that if we do nothing we are also at fault. Action involves personal choices that may be a little painful or uncomfortable to our way of living. The solution to climate chaos is not just technological; it is ethical and religious. It is firstly a moral issue and only then becomes a political and an engineering one. The issue of climate justice is comprehensively and convincingly explained on the website www.mrfc.org/principles.

In *The Brothers Karamazov,* Fydor Dostoyevsky has one of his characters say:

> Love all of God's creation, the whole and every grain of sand in it. Love every leaf, every ray of God's life. Love the animals, love the plants, love everything. If you love

everything, you will perceive the divine in things. Once you have perceived it, you will begin to comprehend it better every day. And you will come at last to love the whole world with an all-embracing love.

# Appendix

WHICH of these responses is closest to your response at the end of Chapter Four?

- *a.* 'I can't believe it.'
- *b.* 'I hope you do.'
- *c.* 'Do you really?'
- *d.* 'Why do you love me?'
- *e.* 'You don't know me.'
- *f.* 'If you really knew me, you wouldn't'
- *g.* 'You're joking.'
- *h.* 'What do you want?'
- *i.* 'Can you prove it?'
- *j.* 'It depends on how close the person is.'
- *k.* 'I love you too.'
- *l.* 'Thank you.'
- *m.* 'That's great! Thank you'
- *n.* 'That makes me really happy. Thank you.'

If your response resembles:

- *a.*   Do you think yourself unlovable?
- *b.* or *c.*   Have you doubts about how lovable you are?
- *d.*   Do you think that love must be earned?
- *e.* or *f.*   Is there something which you think makes you unlovable?
- *g.*   Are you uncomfortable about being loved?
- *h.* or *i.*   Are you suspicious of love until it is clearly proven?

j.    Are you distrustful about accepting love?

k.    Are you in a hurry to return love before you have relished it?

l.    Are you hesitant to relish love before expressing thanks for it?

m. or n.    You have first accepted and enjoyed the gift of love and then said 'thank you'. You have 'opened' your gift, looked at it, relished it and expressed gratitude for it.

# Works Cited

Augustine of Hippo. *Confessions.* Barnes and Noble.

Baba Ram Dass. *Be Here Now* Lama Foundation, 1971

Beecher, Henry Ward, A*utobiography.* Touchstone, an imprint of Simon and Schuster

Berry Thomas. *The Sacred Universe.* Columbia University Press. 2009

Blake William. 'I Sought My Soul', *Poems and Letters.* Abe Books 1777

Bonhoeffer, Dietrich. *The Cost of Discipleship.* Touchstone, an imprint of Simon and Schuster 1995

Benner, Jeff A. *The Ancient Hebrew Lexicon of the Bible*, 2005

Buber, Martin, *I and Thou* Touchstone, an imprint of Simon and Schuster

Burke, Edmund, *Selected Letters.* University of Chicago Press, 1984.

Carrel, Alexis. *Man the Unknown.* Harper and Row, 2013.

Carver, Raymond. *A New Path to the Waterfall.* Atlantic, 1990

Cassidy, Sheila. *Sharing the Darkness.* Darton Longman and Todd. 1988

Clogher Justice, Peace and Integrity of Creation Group, *Climate*

*Change*

Collins, Francis S., *The Question of God.* Free Press. 2017

Craik. Dina Maria. *A Life for a Life.* Atkinson & Co.

Curran, Charles (Ed.), *The Development of Moral Theology.* Georgetown University Press, 2013

Darwin, Charles. *Origin of Species.* Product Dimensions.

De Chardin, Pierre Teilhard. *The Divine Milieu*, Perennial Classics, 2010.

Dostoyevsky Fydor. *The Brothers Karamazov.* Penguin Classics

Einstein, Albert. *The World as I See It.* BN Publishing.1949

Erickson, Erik. *Identity and the Life Cycle.* W.W. Norton & Co. 1959.

Ford, Henry. *My Life and Work.* Doubleday, 1922.

Francis, Pope. *Laudato Si'.* Vatican Polyglot Press. 2015

Frankl, Viktor. *Man's Search for Meaning.* Random Press, 1946.

Frankl, Viktor, *The Unconscious God*, Simon and Schuster, 1975.

Freeman, Dyson. *Dreams of Earth and Sky.* New York Review of Books. 2015

Fromm, Erich. *The Art of Love.* Harper 1956

Fromm, Erich and Adolphe Thiers, *The Sane Society*, Routledge, 1955

Gibram Kahil. *The Prophet.* Alfred A. Knopf, 1923

Grey, Martin. *For Those I Have Loved.* Little, Brown and Company.1990.

Hammarskjold, Dag. *Markings* Faber & Faber.1963.

Huxley, Aldous. *Brave New World.* Harper Perennial. 2006.

Jeffers, Susan. *Feel the Fear and Do It Anyway* Vermilion, 1987

Johnson. Elizabeth. *Ask the Beasts.* Bloomsbury Continuum. 2016

Julian of Norwich. *Revelations of Divine Love.* Penguin Classics 1998.

Kahneman, Daniel. *Thinking Fast and Slow.* Farrar, Straus & Giroux 2011.

Kasper, W. *Mercy*. Paulist Press NY 2013

Kasper, Walter (contributor), *Congress on Mercy*. Vatican Radio, 10 April 2015

Kavanagh, Patrick. *Tarry Flynn*. The Pilot Press, 1948.

Keller Helen. *The Story of My Life*. Cosimo Incorporated 2009.

Kierkegaard, Søren, *Either Or*. Penguin 1843

King, Martin Luther. *Strength to Love*. Harper and Row1963

Lao Tzu. *The Rickshaw Boy*. Harper Collins 2010

Lawrence, D.H. *The Rainbow*. Modern Library. 1915

Levi, Primo. *If This Is a Man*. Onion Press 1959

Lonergan, Bernard.*Method in Theology*. Herder & Herder 1990

May, Gerald. *Care of Mind and of the Spirit*. Harper Collins, 1982

McCabe, Herbert. *God Matters*. Continuum, 1987.

McLaughlin, Nelly. *Out of Wonder*. Veritas. 2015.

Merton, Thomas. *No Man Is an Island*, Harcourt, Brace and Company, 1955

Mill, John Stuart *Autobiography*. Create Space Publishing Co.

Mother Teresa. *A Simple Path*. Liguori Press, 1995

Murray, John Courtney. *We Hold these Truths*. University Press of America 2014.

Nightingale, Florence. *To Her Nurses*. Macmillan & Company 1914

Nin, Anais. *The Diary of Anais Nin*. Mariner Books, 1969

Nussbaum, Martha. *Examined Life*. The New Press 2009.

Peck, Scott, *The Road less Travelled*, Simon and Shuster, 1993.

Peck, Scott *Further Along the Road*. Pocket Books.1993

Rahner, Karl. *A Rahner Reader*. Darton, Longman, Todd. 1975

Reisman, Glazer and Denny. *The Lonely Crowd*. Yale University Press, 1950.

Roethke, Theodore. *Collected Poems*, Bantam Books, 2011.

Russell, Bertrand. *History of Western Philosophy* 1945.

Schweitzer, Albert. *Out of My Life and Thought.* John Hopkins Press, 1923

Sheehy Gail, *Passages*, Ballantine Books, 1995.

St Vincent Millay, Edna. *Collected Works.* Harper and Brothers, 2009

Synod of Bishops, *Justice in the World* 1971

Tagore, Rabindranath. *Selected Letters.* Cambridge University Press, 2016.

Tennyson Alfred. *Poems.* Macmillan and Company.1832.

Thiers, Adolphe and Erich Fromm, *The Sane Society*, Routledge, 1955

Tutu Desmond. *The Book of Joy.* Penguin Random.2016.

Wilson, Bill *Alcoholics Anonymous.* Alcoholics Anonymous World Services, 1939

World Bank Report (2017)